James Redding Ware

The Isle of Wight

James Redding Ware

The Isle of Wight

ISBN/EAN: 9783744724548

Printed in Europe, USA, Canada, Australia, Japan

Cover: Foto ©Thomas Meinert / pixelio.de

More available books at **www.hansebooks.com**

THE

ISLE OF WIGHT.

BY

J. REDDING WARE.

The Photographic Illustrations by

RUSSELL SEDGFIELD AND FRANK M. GOOD.

SECOND EDITION.

London:
PROVOST & CO.,
36, HENRIETTA STREET, COVENT GARDEN.
1871.

Contents.

	PAGE
Introduction	1
Geology of the Isle	4
Bird's-eye View and General Description	11
Political History	21
The History from the date of Annexation to England	44
Ryde	66
Brading	82
Quarr Abbey	91
East and West Cowes	96
Osborne	102
Newport...	107
Shanklin	122
Luccombe Chine	128
The Undercliff	129
Bonchurch	133
Ventnor	137
St. Lawrence	140
Blackgang Chine	144
Carisbrook and its Castle	151
Environs of Carisbrook, &c...	166
Shorwell...	169
Freshwater Bay	171
Scratchell's Bay	175
Yarmouth	179

LIST OF PHOTOGRAPHS.

Brading	By RUSSELL SEDGFIELD	Frontispiece
		PAGE
The Needles ...	„ FRANK M. GOOD	... 12
Godshill ...	„ RUSSELL SEDGFIELD ...	63
Ryde	„ „ ...	66
Cowes	From a Painting	97
Osborne... ...	By RUSSELL SEDGFIELD	103
Shanklin Chine ...	„ „ ...	122
Shanklin Church ...	„ „	... 125
Boncburch .	„ „	133
Ventnor ...	„ „	137
Blackgang Chine ...	„ FRANK M. GOOD	144
Carisbrook Castle	„ RUSSELL SEDGFIELD ...	... 151
Shorwell ...	„ „	170
Freshwater Bay	„ „	171
Scratchell's Bay	„ FRANK M. GOOD ...	175

Introduction.

THE Ifle of Wight is the paradife of bees, flowers, and invalids. Almoft throughout the year there are blofloms for the buzzing bees, who are awake and careering through the air long after their Englifh brethren have said " good-night " to the year and have hived themfelves accordingly. Even into December, that ufually chilly month (though perhaps, in its early days only), invalids have been known to take conftitutionals accompanied by para-sols and umbrellas, thefe conftitutionals being taken in the moft nooky parts of fuch a natural winter-garden as the unequaled Ventnor. The iflanders are perfectly aware of the rarity, the exceptional quality of their climate, and indeed they do not take the need-lefs trouble to praife it very much. The ifland fpeaks for itfelf. Storms are pofitively rare in the Isle of Wight.

But while the iflanders are prone to attribute this fatisfactory ftate of meteorological things to something very much in the

B

nature of special provifion, the lefs enthufiaftic ftranger is prompted to queftion fcience upon this point, only, however, to afcertain that fcience has no reply whatever to make.

But little attention has been given to the confideration of this fubject, and it muft be left to future phyfical geographers and meteorologifts to analyfe the queftion.

The changes in paffing round the Ifle of Wight are moft infinite. To the north the fhores are generally low and inclined towards the main land, for it is here the greedy fea fwept into the land, and cut away the ifland from England. Here, on the north, between Hampfhire and the ifle the fea has fapped and melted away the land in fweet fummer weather; here in winter the high and feething waters have bitten out huge titanic mouthfuls, sucking, undermining, rending. The foft, marfhy land has yielded without any refiftance beyond its weight and its extent. From the time when the fea at laft feparated the land, and fwept round it, another ifland, the water has never ceafed to abforb the weak ftrata lying along the north fhore. As you walk you can fee the land yielding. Hark! a fplafh, although the fea is only whifpering to the faint breeze, and not a human found comes near you. It is a piece of the foil yielded to its implacable enemy—the fea; and if you watch, you will mark how the almoft motionlefs water will melt away and flowly level it.

Examine well the yielding land upon the north of the ifland. Mark the fiffures in the foft earth. Here is a wild rofe growing half on one fide of a crack, half on the other. The flow fummer fea has undermined the ground it grew upon, and the roots are feparating. A few days, and with another foft plunge and fplafh, half the wild rofe bufh will be engulfed. It will be the turn of the other half this year, or the year that is to come.

Look away a yard over the water. There you fee a cake of earth, with this year's leaves ftill flourifhing, albeit the mother-earth has been fwept to fea. How long will the leaves twitter in the breeze? If the waves rife angrily, the tiny blofToming ifland will be fwept away to-night; if not to-night, to-morrow.

Look farther, and you will fee laft year's branches below the water, ftill clinging to the fubmerged ground. The branches now bear other fruit than blackberries, hips, and haws; amongft them floats other life than gnat and midge. Tiny little mollufcs have fixed upon the twigs; they are the young fry of the *frutti del' mare*, of the fea-fruit that men gather in nets. And in place of the midges you may mark tiny atoms of life floating in and out, and playing at that ceafelefs game of catch-catch which the summer flies keep up through all the hours of the day.

There is the tiny world below the water, drawing the lines of its univerfe at high water-mark; and at a diftance fo narrow that it evades meafurement. On the very furface of the water itfelf begins the life of the air. And between the two is the land, ceafelefsly yielding to the unceafing fea, and after ferving the life of the air through ages—a moment, and yielding to the water, it becomes the immediate home of new fhapes of life.

But on the fouth fide of the ifle the land has warred with the water, and difputed every grain of chalk or ftone. On the north, the angry fea fweeps over the land, ravening and tearing it away. On the fouth, the high proud cliffs drive back the imperious water, which, repelled, will rife in its frothing rage high, it is faid, as any lighthoufe there.

The fea can wait. The cliffs refift, but they muft yield in immenfe lengths of time. For months, for years, the waters may boil round the Needle rocks, and only a whitened water

fhall be the refult, as though the fea had turned pale with rage
at its ineffectual attacks; when, fuddenly, a mighty wave beats
at the rock, and over it heels, the water leaping and screaming
athwart it like a thing of life. Then apparently, the waters
are appeafed. Information of the change in the afpect of the
Needles is fent up to the Trinity Houfe; sailors grow accus-
tomed to their new form; and the old fhape is almoft
forgotten, only to be recalled when again the fea claims
another rock.

Within the memory of many of the iflanders the afpect
of the Needles has changed more than once.

Some day, in a mighty ftorm, fuch as appears to rage only
once in the courfe of centuries, the whole line of rocks
called the Needles will be fwept away, the cliffs will fall,
woods will be engulfed, and a new view of the ifland will
be created.

The fea is never ftill, never fatiated, and though the land
refifts, it is ever yielding bit by bit.

How long fhall it be before the fea will fwallow the cliffs
which ftill defy it? Many thoufands of years may pafs before
the cliff above Scratchell's Bay falls, but the cave now being
fcooped into the chalk tells how, in time to come, down muft
fall that mighty rock.

Mantell, in his charming book devoted to the geology of the
Ifle of Wight, has given feveral pages to an analyfis of the
geology from Ryde to Alum Bay—that greateft wonder of the
Ifle. He fays, " The fteam-packets from Ryde to Yarmouth
pafs fufficiently near the northern fhore of the ifland to afford a
general view of the outcrop of the ftrata in the cliffs and bays
formed by the inroads of the fea, and at the mouths of the
rivers and eftuaries. The coaft from Ryde to Cowes exhibits
little or no feature of geologic intereft. Here and there flips

or fubfidences in the low cliffs have expofed beds of calcareous marl and frefh-water limeftone, covered by alluvial clay and loam, along the fea-bounds of Her Majefty's eftate at Ofborne, and of the grounds of Norris Caftle. Along the fhore, at low water, numerous foffils and fhells, which have been wafhed up, are very often to be met with.

"On the north fide of Garnet Bay, about two miles weft of Cowes, the cliffs are compofed of alternating beds of clay and limeftone, the latter abounding in frefh-water fhells. In Thorley Bay fimilar ftrata are obferved, with layers of blue clay and fand, containing marine fhells. In feveral localities along the whole north fhore of the ifle, fluvio-marine clays appear on the fides of the floping banks, but the exact ftratigraphical pofition of thefe beds is concealed by vegetation. They are probably the equivalents of the ftrata at the northern end of Whitecliff Bay, which contain an intermixture of marine and fluviatile fhells.

"Beyond Newtown Bay are Hampftead Cliffs, about nine miles eaft of Yarmouth, confifting of calcareous marls, with the ufual fluviatile fhells in great abundance.

"Paffing Yarmouth, and reaching the fhore oppofite Hurft Caftle, we enter Colwell Bay, where the cliffs exhibit an alternation of marine and frefh-water ftrata. In the fiffure called Bramble Chine a thick bed of oyfter fhells is expofed, apparently in its original ftate, the valves being in contact with each other as when the mollufcs were living. This appears to be the equivalent of the oyfter-bed obfervable in Whitecliff Bay. Many beautiful foffil fhells may be collected in this locality. In Totland, or Tolland's Bay—the latter title being a corruption—fimilar fands, clays, and marls form the cliffs. Thence we reach Alum Bay."

. To our thinking, the wonderful parti-coloured fand and

clay cliffs, in vertical ftrata, of Alum Bay form the moft
wondrous and beautiful geological puzzle that is to be found in
the world of geology.   No geologift has attempted to account
for the ever-varying changes in colour of the fand-layers, fome
of which are fo thin that they appear to be the work of only a
few minutes' depofit.

Of the ftriped Alum Bay cliffs—from an artiftic point of
view—it can only be faid that they are fimply beyond praife.
Their appearance has been compared to a filk of banded
colours.   The harmony and variety of their tones, their
combined beauty, their foft fhadows, their interminable changes
grow upon you much after the fafhion of one of Turner's
more recondite pictures.   Then again, the play of light and
fhade upon the broken furface multiplies the tints a thoufand
fold.   There is no geologic example in the whole world fimilar
to this ftriped cliff phenomenon in Alum Bay, of the rationale
of which all geologifts appear to be in abfolute ignorance, fince
they make no attempt to explain the puzzle.   It is a beautiful
myftery.

And another ftrange thing about thefe varied fands is this,
that as they mix at the bottom of the glorious cliff, they mingle
into the ordinary tone of fea-fand, and refemble that here found
upon the beach, and from which fo good a glafs is made.

The courfe of thefe parti-coloured fands may be followed as
far as Frefhwater, where, haply digging a hole in a hedge, a
ftream of rofe-coloured fand fhall flow forth as though there
were magic in it.

Mantell grows enthufiaftic in defcribing Alum Bay :—
" The panorama prefented by the fweep of Alum Bay is
quite unequalled throughout the ifland, and probably is not, for
equal peculiarity and beauty, furpaffed by any ftretch of coaft
line in the United Kingdom."

Sir Henry Englefield, an amateur geologist, defcribes the fpot in the following language :—" The fcenery of this Bay is very fuperior to that of any other part of the ifland. The chalk forms an unbroken face everywhere, nearly perpendicular, in fome parts moft formidably projecting, and the tendereft ftains of ochrous yellow and greenifh moift vegetation vary without breaking its fublime uniformity. This vaft wall extends nearly a quarter of a mile, is more than four hundred feet in height, and terminates by a thin projection with a bold broken outline. And the wedge-fhaped Needle Rocks, rifing out of the blue waters, continue the cliff in idea beyond its prefent boundary, giving an awful impreffion of the ftormy ages which have gradually devoured its enormous mafs. The pearly hue of the chalk under certain conditions of the atmofphere and light is beyond defcription by words, and probably out of the power of the pencil to pourtray. The magical repofe of this fide of the bay is wonderfully contrafted by the torn forms and vivid colouring of the cliffs on the oppofite fide. Thefe do not, as at Whitecliff, prefent rounded headlands clothed with turf and fhrubs, but offer a feries of points of a fcalloped form, and which are often fharp and pinnacled. Deep, rugged chafms divide the ftrata in many places, and not a trace of vegetation appears in any part; all is wild ruin. The tints of the cliffs are fo bright and varied that they have not the aspect of anything natural. Deep purplifh red, dufky blue, bright ochreous yellow, grey nearly approaching to white, and abfolute black, fucceed each other as clearly defined as the ftripes in filk; while, after rains, the fun, which, in fummer, from about noon to his fetting, increafingly illuminates them, gives a brilliancy to fome of thefe ftrata nearly as refplendent as the lights on real filk. Small veffels often lie in this bay for the purpofe of loading chalk and fand, and they ferve admirably to fhow the majeftic fize of the cliffs, under whofe fhade they lie diminifhed almoft to nothing."

Continuing his analyfis of the geology of the coaft line at and about Alum Bay, Mantell says :—" Although the uncon-formable pofition and diflocated ftrata at Headon Hill appear at firft fight to prefent little correfpondence with the nearly horizontal frefh-water depofits at Whitecliff Bay, and the richly coloured and variegated ftripes of fands and clays on the vertical cliffs of Alum Bay, ftill lefs to refemble the dull, ochreous marine beds expofed in the breaks of the turf-covered flopes of that locality, yet a careful examination will foon convince the obferver that the geological characters of this north-weftern fection of the eocene ftrata agree in every effential feature with thofe which fhould engage his attention at the eaftern extremity of the ifland. The variegated and deeply-tinted fands, marls, and clays, which impart fo remarkable and brilliant an afpect to the cliff, are between feven and eight hundred feet high. The attenuations and variety of the vertical feams or layers are almoft innumerable. The fands are of every fhade, of red, yellow, green, and grey. Some are white, and others almoft black. The clays are equally diverfified."

Mr. Webfter, another hiftorian of the ifle, remarks :— " The variety of the vertical layers is endlefs, and may be com-pared to the ftripes of a parti-coloured tulip. On cutting down pieces of the cliff, it is aftonifhing to fee the brightnefs of the colours and the delicacy and thinnefs of the feveral layers of the white and red fand, fhale and white fand, yellow clay and white and red fand, and indeed almoft every imaginable com-bination of thefe materials. In the midft of this feries there are vertical layers of pebbles, and one thick ftratum, and many feams of lignite."

This lignite, it appears to us, points to coal, which has been
found and worked on the ifland, but to an unprofitable conclufion.　Alum Bay takes its name, it is ufually faid, from
alum having been found on the beach.　However this may be,
its coloured fands are certainly the wonder of the Ifle of
Wight.　Seen from the water at funfet, their wealth of colour,
of mingled light and fhadow, is quite beyond any attempt at
defcription.

And there is another peculiarity to be noticed at Alum Bay,
a peculiar pearlinefs of the chalk cliffs which furround the
bay—this phenomenon being feen at certain times and feafons;
indeed, at all times there is a fingular chiarofcuro to be obferved
in connection with them.　Mantell ("*Geological Excurfions
round the Ifle of Wight*")—and his work is the moft charming
book upon geology which has yet been written—quitting the
coaft line, and turning inland says, fpeaking of the towering
downs :—"We fee two parallel fweeps of huge hills, ftretching
eaft and weft along the whole length of the fea-bound landfcape.
The northern range claims only moderate height, and flopes
gradually to the fhore, while it exhibits that fmoothened,
rounded, circle-cutting-circle outline, which at once tells the
geologift, whatever the embroidery fuch a landfcape may have
upon it, foreft, grafs, corn, or heather, that the formation is
pure white chalk.　The firft line of hills confifts," fays our
author, " of frefh-water ftrata, which are fuper-impofed on the
eocene marine depofits.　The fouthern range of hills claims
the greater altitude, the greater length ; each point feems
to be ftretching higher than its neighbour, and this rivalry
may be marked fairly along the whole length of the ifland,
from the eaft promontory of Culver Cliffs to the extreme
weftern Needles."

Of the geological formation of the fouthern hills, Mr.

c

Mantell fays:—"The fouthern divifion is almoft entirely compofed of the different members of the cretaceous fyftem. The white chalk forms a range of domes from the eaftern to the weftern extremity, and is flanked on the fouth by the lower beds of this formation. Thefe are fucceeded by another group of chalk hills that expands into a broad and lofty promontory, in fome parts between eight hundred and nine hundred feet high, headed by St. Catherine's, Shanklin, and Boniface Downs. On the fouthern efcarpment of this chain the upper depofits of the cretaceous fyftem reappear, and fallen maffes of thefe rocks form the irregular line of terraces which conftitute the Undercliff. The downs on the fouthern coaft are feparated from thofe inland by an anticlinal axis, which extends through this part of the ifland, and is produced by the upheaval of the fire-ftone, gault, and green fand. The promontory of the Undercliff is flanked both on the eaft and weft by extenfive bays, which have been excavated in the clay and fands of the Wealden and inferior cretaceous depofits by the long-continued fapping of the fea. The Wealden occupies an inconfiderable extent of furface; but in Sandown Bay on the eaft, and in Brixton, Brook, and Compton Bays on the weft, the cliffs, which are formed of the upper clays and fands of this formation, are expofed to unremitting deftruction from the action of the waves. The fea-fhore is therefore ftrewn with the detritus of thefe fluviatile ftrata, and the fhingle contains innumerable water-worn fragments of the bones of reptiles and other organic remains."

The geology of the Ifle of Wight is by no means wanting in majefty. A ftudent who defires to make himfelf mafter of this fubject will find Mantell an invaluable guide.

A Bird's-eye View and General Defcription of the Ifle.

——◦◦◦——

IT is from the higheft of the downs in the Ifle of Wight that a bird's-eye view of the ifle is obtained. Thefe downs or hill ranges vary from four hundred to feven hundred feet in height, while one line of hills runs through the ifland "like a back-bone." It is this back-bone which offers, when it is furmounted, as glorious a view as any in the whole fouth of England. Standing on Arreton Down, and looking north-weft, the eyes mark on one fide the peaceful palace of Her Majefty, on the other the remains of the warlike old caftle of Carifbrook, with its now ufelefs loop-holes, and its ramparts covered by nature with that type of civilization—ivy, which creeps over old caftle and abbey, an ever frefh fermon upon the vanity of overftrained power. Men have built to control and defy. Control has been loft, and defiance is in the duft, and here is the ivy curtaining the proud ftone-work.

Below Carifbrook Caftle is the metropolis, as we fuppofe it muft be called, Newport; and lying above it the inevitable prifon, backed by the heavy folid depths of Parkhurft Foreft. Away, on the horizon, may be feen the downs above the Needles, high and towering, and feeming, when feen from the fhell of fome fmall boat a mile or two at fea, veritable mountains. Of thefe rocks—the Land's End of the Ifle of Wight—the Rev. W. L. Bowles has fung :—

> " On thefe white cliffs, that, calm above the flood,
>   Uplift their fhadowing heads, and, at their feet,
>   Scarce hear the furge that has for ages beat,
> Here many a lonely wanderer has ftood;
> And, whilft the lifted murmur met his ear,
>   And o'er the diftant billows the ftill eve
>   Sailed flow, has thought of all his heart muft leave
> To-morrow ; of the friends he loved moft dear ;
> Of focial fcenes, from which he wept to part,
>   But if, like me, he knew how fruitlefs all
>   The thoughts that would full fain the paft recall,
> Soon would he quell the rifings of his heart,
> And brave the wild winds and unhearing tide,
> The world his country, and his God his guide."

A writer, referring to the Needles, very juftly says :— " From the chalky nature of this remarkable group of rocks, and of the coaft of the ifland from which they have been detached, continual changes are taking place in their form and difpofition. In fome places the fea has eaten through them, and formed large and irregular archways ; in others, it has fo wafhed away their fides, that they look rather like walls than folid rocks; while deep caverns have been formed in the cliffs which fall in from time to time, and gradually diminifh the ifland in that direction."

Old records of Wight, by the way, teem with ftatements of the abundance of wild fowl in this part of the ifle.

The Needles are now as unlike needles as they well can be,

THE NEEDLES FROM SCRATCHELL'S BAY

for they are almoft as broad at their fummits as their bafes. But an engraving made even fo late as 1832–1840, gives the whole range a diftinctly pointed character.

Let us fweep round towards the balmy fouth, and we fhall fee the cheery-looking Frefhwater Bay, made claffic by the refidence of Tennyfon on the hill above, and charming in itfelf by the bounty of nature. Now bring the eyes along the coaft line of chines, themfelves a marvel of contraftive ftudy, and—you mark that point!—the Under-cliff, which like a guardian angel, hides white-houfed and parapet-like Ventnor from the view. But you may mark the thin white fmoke rifing in the air. Still drift along the coaft line: your eyes are now glancing over the beautiful valley of the ifland—the fruitful valley, wherein neftles Arreton, and where is harvefted more than the iflanders can confume.

Elizabeth Wallbridge, a pious peafant girl, whofe hiftory has been fimply and feelingly narrated by the Rev. Legh Richmond, in a fmall volume entitled " The Dairyman's Daughter," was born in Arreton, and lies interred in the churchyard.

The church was one of thofe given to the Abbey of Lyra, by William Fitz-William ; and, in the reign of Henry I., when Baldwin de Redvers endowed the Abbey of Quarr, he either gave the manor of Arreton, or procured it for his new foundation, to which it belonged till the abbey was diffolved. The church, which is dedicated to St. George, is an ancient edifice, confifting of a nave and chancel, with a fouth aifle. In the aifle, is an ancient plate of brafs, on which is the effigy of a man in armour, with his feet on a lion ; and underneath is this infcription :—

Here is y buried: under this graue,
Harry Hawles: his soule God saue:
Longe tyme steward: of the Jle of Wyght:
Haue mcy on hym: God ful of myght.

There are alfo fome handfome monuments to the Holmes family; that to Sir Leonard Worsley Holmes is peculiarly worthy of attention; the fculptor, Mr. Hafkoll, was a native of the ifland.

Arreton Farm-houfe is a good fpecimen of the Jacobean domeftic architecture.

From Arreton Down may be enjoyed a profpect of wonderful beauty,—hamlets fhining among leafy copfes, venerable manor-houfes and ancient farmfteads, meadows and uplands, ftreams, groves, and fhadowy combes. On its fummit a few years ago, two confiderable *tumuli*, or barrows were opened, and many interefting relics exhumed. St. George's Down is quite claffic ground. Here, in the days of the Earl of Southampton (1607–9), was a famous bowling green, "railed in" at the coft of the gentry of the ifland, and a fort of fummer-houfe, maintained in a bountiful fafhion. "I have feen," fays Sir John Oglander, "with my Lord of Southampton at St. George's Down, at bowls, some thirty or forty knights and gentlemen, where our meeting was then twice every week, Tuefdays and Thurfdays; and we had an ordinary there, and card-tables." Wyndham fays, "This is the moft centric elevation of the ifland. It is unconnected with any other hills, and the plain upon its top may be a mile in length. The views from it are not fo exclufive as thofe from the higher hills, though they are fufficiently varied to arreft, occafionally, the progrefs of a paffenger, and, particularly, on the fpot where the whole length of the Newport river difclofes itfelf, from that low town even to the harbour and ftreets of Cowes."

Now let us return to our bird's-eye view.

To your left is Brading Harbour, honoured by the memory of noble Sir Hugh Myddleton, who tried fo bravely to give London good water. And now another turn will bring Ryde and Cowes into view. And thus in a few fentences, we have carried you round the ifland, and given you a bird's-eye view from one of its higheft points. And thus having, after a manner, introduced you to the Ifle of Wight, you will permit us to come down from our ftand-point.

The principal river, and it is not a very wide one, is the Medina, from the Latin *Medius* it is faid. This river very fairly divides the ifland into halves, to which have been given the diftinctive titles, east and weft Medina. But we may add that when the guide-books defcribe the Medina as dividing the ifland into halves, it muft not thereupon be fuppofed that there are two Ifles of Wight. In fact the river only cleaves the ifland at its wideft part one third of its width. However, if a line be taken fouth from the rife of the Medina, and in continuation of the direction of the river, which flows due north, it will certainly very fairly make the divifion roughly defcribed to be achieved by the one water-way to which the iflanders have the hardi-hood to apply the term river. To be fure there is the eaftern Yar, flowing into the almoft-lake called Brading Harbour, and the weftern Yar (for it is a peculiarity of the ifland that what-ever place there is on the weftern fide is duplicated in name on the eaftern, of courfe with the fubftitution of eaftern for weftern) which flows into the Solent at Yarmouth. In neither cafe can the ftranger quite tell where the river is, and when he has found it he difcovers that, a lateral brook or two apart, he has arrived at the fource. But the rational tourift cannot expect to find Miffouries and Miffiffippis in an ifland which is only fixty miles in circumference.

The weftern Yar forms Frefhwater into a peninfula. In fact, the Isle of Wight is quite a primitive leffon in phyfical geography, while at the fame time the hiftory of its political geography is abforbing in intereft.

But though the ifland is charming in itfelf, it is looked upon
with gravity by all paffing mariners. Bembridge Point, the
Foreland, Dunnofe, Eaft End, Rocken End, St. Catherine
Point, Atherfield Point, Brook Point, the Needles, and
Headon Hill—thefe are words affociated with fearful wrecks
and hair-breadth efcapes, to the lift of which every winter
throws its fearful contribution.

Perhaps the moft remarkable and diftinctive landfcape
features of the ifle are the chines, a difagreeable term, but one
pre-eminently forcible. There has been fo much wordy con-
teft over the derivation of this defignation, that it is only wifely
judicious to maintain filence upon the point. Charles Knight
paffes by the queftion to describe the natural object itfelf. That
lucid writer fays, "The chines are deep fiffures which have
been cut in the cliffs by the action of a ftreamlet falling over
the fummit. All of them have the fame general features.
There is a wide opening feaward which contracts inland with
more or lefs rapidity, according to the hardnefs of the rock, the
greater or lefs quantity of water which ordinarily falls over, or
other circumftances. In fome cafes the ravine reaches for
nearly a mile inland, and is loft at length in the ordinary bed of
the brook; in others, it terminates abruptly in a waterfall.
Although the ftream muft in every inftance be regarded as the
chief agent in cutting the chine, its enlargement is perhaps as
much, or more, owing to other influences. The action of the
waves during great ftorms, when the fea is driven violentl; againft
the cliffs, has tended confiderably to enlarge the opening of the
chines, while the landflips, which continually occur after fevere
frofts, muft have caufed the fteep flopes to fall in from time to time.
But the deepening of the chines is always brought about by the
ftream, as may be obferved in any of them where meafures are
not taken to prevent the conftant wearing away of the rock."

But no human meafures can in the wealth of time prevent nature from her work. A fkilful wall, a well-made brick-built water-way, may arreft the eating down of the land by the running water, but it will laft only a hundred years or two, and then patient nature will again work on.

But it is the botanift, the being who in friendly oppofition to the geologift, feeks the lateft of heaven's work, as the geologift—and all honour to him—feeks the earlieft, who will find in the Ifle of Wight that he has been very fpecially provided for. Very early in the fpring, and only two hours' journey away from Hampfhire, he may find fnowdrops and crocufes in full bloom, when on the main-land thofe daring flowers, with all their courage, have not ventured to raife their heads. A little later in the fpring, when not a leaf is fairly out upon even the fycamore tree, fhrubberies will be found radiant with little floral ftars, for the greater part white, and often the ground will be all a-tangle with wild ftrawberry, while the primrofes have grown fo large on all fides that they feem to be flowers which have come of age.

It may be faid of the Ifle of Wight, that here you may find examples of the entire Englifh flora, if not even of the floras of Wales, Ireland, and Scotland, with one of its own added. Efpecially are the ordinary fea-beach and fea-fide hill flowers to be found in perfection.

Flowers fcarcely know what winter means in the ifle. When nature has retired for the feafon in England, and mats are being put about pet plants in the neighbourhood of places even fo foutherly as London and Canterbury, away in the more favoured parts of the ifle, fuchfia, geranium, and myrtle are ftill throwing out bloom. Indeed, flowering plants appear to think that their hardeft working time of the year is about the period when, in other localities, vegetation,

except of a very ordinary and market-gardening character,
is going to reſt. You get wild flowers, dale flowers, hedge
flowers, foreſt flowers, ſand flowers, creepers innumerable,
and ivy beyond convenience. Leaves on the trees are
thicker than elſewhere, nettles grow higher; you may find
heather on the broken downs; and now and again a ſharp-eyed
botaniſt goes to the iſle and is ſure to find one or two new varieties
which have never been ſeen there before, and which have not
been found in any other part of the United Kingdom.

Here we cannot enumerate the wonders of the Iſle of Wight
flora; we refer our readers to the *Flora Veĉtenſis* of Dr. Bromfield,
whoſe work has been edited and added to by Dr. Bell Salter.
But a few revelling ſentences may be permitted us. A
botaniſt, or rather a floriſt—for the iſle is rather the ſublunary
heaven of the lover of flowers than the devotee of plants—
will read the following lines with much the ſame reliſh that a
judge of wines will read the cellar-book of a great wine collector.

Does the reader devote himſelf or herſelf to Botany? Then
let him ſeek the neighbourhood of Rookley, Freſhwater,
Alverſtone, Thorley, Shanklin, Quarr, and Cariſbrook. There
may be found the *Oſmunda*, the *Bog-pimpernel*, and *Bog-
aſphodel; Utricularia minor* (near Newchurch); *Utricularia
major* (Freſhwater marſhes); *Trichomanes* (Cariſbrook and
Quarr); the *Adder's Tongue* (Thorley and Eaſt End); and
Ruta Muraria (Freſhwater and Calbourne).

Cloſe in by the ſea, between Ryde and Sandown, one
is certain, at the fit and proper times, to be hailed by the
Sea-ſide Ruſh, Drop-wort, the *Smooth Sea-heath, Sea-holly,
Yellow Centaury, Sea Mat-graſs,* and *Nottingham Catch-fly.*

Go to Newport and Cariſbrook, and you will certainly find
*Arabis Hirſuta, Red-berried Briony, Autumnal Gentian,
Grammitis Ceterach, Leaſt Toad-flax,* and *Butcher's Broom.*

At Culver Cliffs are found the *Portland Sponge* and *Orobanche* (*Broom-rape*); at Binftead. the *Broad-leaved Helleborine;* upon the downs around Ventnor the *Orchides* (*Ophrys Apifera* and *Ophrys Mufcifera*); and the *Bee-Orchis* may be gathered at Quarr and Binftead.

" From the variety," fays an eminent phyfician, " which the Ifle of Wight prefents in point of elevation, foil, and afpect, and from the configuration of its hills and fhores, it poffeffes all things that can render it a highly favourable refidence for an invalid, and a habitat for innumerable flowers."

Poets, doctors, florifts, tourifts, all combine in unceafingly praifing the Ifle of Wight.

It has a metropolis, of courfe—Newport ; and the number of parifhes in the two Medinas is——but of what avail fhall it be that the reader learn the number of parifhes ? He would forget the numerals before he had turned the leaf.

It is more to the purpofe to point out that, culminating all its natural advantages, the Ifle of Wight poffeffes a " Governor of the Ifland." But it muft be conceded that his duties are merely nominal, for the age is againft fmall governments, divided authorities, and its powerful neighbour the county of Southampton, otherwife Hampfhire, has abforbed the ifle for " all general purpofes," as they exprefs it in the infula. However, the Ifle of Wight returns two members to Parliament— one for the ifland, and one for Newport.

Of the principal towns we fhall have to fay fomething in chapters methodically devoted to each; but we may at once add, that the Ifle of Wight is a perfect little community in itfelf. It not only poffeffes its governor, but it has its municipal organifation, its prifon, its poor-houfe—euphonioufly called " The Houfe of Induftry,"—and its military eftablifhments. No lefs than three thoufand foldiers form the complement at Park-

hurſt barracks.   The coaſt-line is dotted with forts, the greater
number uſeleſs, while perhaps the fineſt, and at the ſame time
uſeful military work completed within the Iſland boundaries
conſiſts of the ſplendid, direct, and ſcientific military highway
running along the ſouthern length of the iſland from Freſhwater
Bay to the out-crop of the Undercliff.   It was this part of the
iſland which was unfortified.   Portſmouth protected an
approach by way of Spithead; Hurſt Caſtle and Yarmouth
forts any advance upon Portſmouth through the Solent ; while
the Undercliff was a natural protection half-a-ſcore of miles in
extent.   Brading, and the downs above it, protected the eaſt
of the iſland.   Only the frequently ſloping land between
Freſhwater and Ventnor was utterly unprotected.   During the
time of the invaſion panic, now ſeven or eight years ſince,
ſhrewd military men recalled to their memories how, in a
comparatively recent—certainly within the modern hiſtoric—
period, the iſle had been held by an enemy, and the ſcheme of
the military road was brought forward and put into execution.
It was accompliſhed with marvellous rapidity.   Certainly it
blocked the weak point in the Engliſh line of ſouthern fortifications.   A hoſtile army, once poſſeſſed of the Iſle of Wight,
a march to Ryde would place it within five miles of the great
arſenal at Portſmouth.   The formation of this road was, therefore, the reſult of a maſterly idea.   The road is not uſeleſs, though
fortunately it has never been applied to what may be called its
legitimate uſes, ſince it forms a new direct road for the farmers.
And this in itſelf is a benefit.   Indeed the Iſle of Wight,
looked at from a military point of view, is now merely an out-
work to Portſmouth.   But we prefer to look upon it from a more
peaceful ſtand-point, and regard it not as a field for warfare, but
as the flower-garden and convaleſcent hoſpital of all England.

Some Account of the Political History of the Isle of Wight.

——◦◦◦——

WHEN the antiquaries have eſſayed to ſettle the derivation of the word Wight, the variation of opinion has been, as it remains, moſt ſtartling. The ordinary man, who has thought upon the ſubjeƈt, has often arrived at the concluſion, that the iſland being more or leſs ſurrounded by high cliffs of dazzling white chalk, the iſle gained its name Wight thereby, ſome allowance being made for orthography, ſeeing that white muſt be a very old Engliſh word, ſimply becauſe the names of colours are amongſt the firſt to be formed in a language, and the laſt to be loſt. And this ſingle argument might be ſtrengthened by the recolleƈtion that England is abroad, very generally called Albion, owing to the dazzlingly white aſpeƈt afforded by thoſe ſouthern cliffs which are the firſt ſpecimens of the country preſented to the foreign view.

But the antiquaries have permitted no fuch fimple derivation to fatisfy them. The Romans called the ifland Vecta, or Vectis, and the antiquaries maintain that Vecta has been corrupted into Wight. They will not hear of the fuggeftion, that probably Cæfar and his followers and fucceffors may have corrupted Wight into Vecta; a corruption which would be much after the procefs by the ufe of which our land came to be called Britannia.

Other antiquaries hold that Wight comes from an old Britifh word, Guith, pronounced probably like " white," and which meant a breach or divifion, in this cafe referring to the fea dividing the ifle from the mainland. But under thefe circumftances it is difficult to comprehend why the term was not applied to the channel rather than the ifland. Both antiquarian fides, however, are agreed that the arguments of each are fupported by the entries in reference to the ifland which are to be found in "Domefday Book," where the reader has the choice between Wect, With, or Wict, a variety which is a good example of what corruption in pronunciation will effect even in one generation. It fhould however be urged that probably thefe three variations in the fpelling of the name of this ifland were almoft fymphonious; the firft, no doubt, was pronounced " Wet," the fecond and third " White."

Antiquarianifm, like moft other fciences, is continually drifting towards fimplicity, and therefore we need have little hefitation in urging that the primitive name of the ifland, given to it by that wonderful exodus of peoples from various points on the fhores of the Mediterranean, which flowed up the outer coaft of Spain, Portugal, and France, and thence peopled the Britifh Ifles, gave, in the firft place, as a maritime people, a name, the equivalent of our " white," to the ifland, a term the refult of the firft obfervation made by thofe early navigators whofe defcendants we in a great meafure muſt be. We may fairly believe that however the name may have been fpelt, through Roman, Saxon, Norman, and Englifh ages, the pronunciation has always been " white." Primitive names fhould be the landmarks of the antiquary. Amongſt primitive names, thofe of hills, rivers, and iflands are moſt marked for their perfiftency. The word *"pen"* (hill or mountain,) is ftill ufed over the whole of that portion of Europe where the races found by the invading North European had placed their feet. We poffefs a very ſtriking and fingularly recent example of a defignation adhering to a great phyfical outline, defpite the influx of new races. The names of almoft all the North American rivers, and of many of the States, remain Indian, albeit in many States the Indian blood has utterly ceafed to circulate. Miffiffippi, Miffouri, Ohio, Maffachufetts —all thefe names are purely Indian. Who can fuppofe that upon the tongues of the millions thefe names can be changed?

Upon thefe arguments we bafe this claim—that the Ifle of Wight retains the name given it by the firft human race which landed upon its fhores and peopled it—an out-going, fea-loving, blue-eyed race, who faw that the ifland was white, and called it " Wight."

It does not appear to be known when the feparation between the ifland and the mainland took place, a feparation which after years of patient working may have been made in a fingle night. But it is juft poffible that the converfion of the peninfula of Wight into the Ifle of Wight may have been effected by the mighty ftorm which fwept along the Channel in 709. In that fearful cataftrophe, Jerfey, which was then a peninfula joined to the coaft by feven miles of ifthmus, in parts two to three miles wide, became an ifland in one night. The ftretch of feven miles was engulfed only to the depth of fome few feet, but

the fea gained its victory. Once England muft have been
wrefted in a fimilar manner from Europe, at the point where
a line would ftretch between Dover and Calais. Only half a
century ago, a fhell-encrufted bank, feen diftinctly in the
fhallow water, marked the place of a row of trees, which in
709 fringed a brook drowned in that great ftorm, which divided
France from the feudal holding of Jerfey. This row of trees
formed the boundary line, feparating the Jerfey from the
Norman fifheries ; and only half a century fince, or a little
more, in a great law-fuit between the Jerfey and the Normandy
fifhermen, in a French law court, this veritable old boundary
line below the fea was brought forward as a natural witnefs
againft the encroaching French fifhermen. The Jerfey netmen
won the day, and to this hour they maintain their rights,
founded upon a bank of fea-fhells formed over a row of trees
which was carried down into the fea more than a thoufand years
ago. Suffice it to learn, that in fome mighty convulfion of
nature, the fea, poffibly combined with volcanic action, did over-
whelm the ifthmus connecting the now Ifle of Wight with the
Englifh foil, and feparated it from the mother-land for ever.

" Art," fays an author, writing of the ifle—" Art, here, as
in fome other cafes, yields to nature the palm of fuperiority.
Nay, fo perfect is nature in thefe parts, that it is maintained
the rate of mortality amongft thofe born on the ifland, living
and dying there, is lower than of any fpot in the United
Kingdom. The general returns, however, including deaths of
invalids, or of people who have taken up their abode in the ifle
as a forlorn hope, to obtain a little longer leafe of life, bring up
the death per centage to quite the average for the whole of
England. The true Wightman is very much hurt in his felf-
love by this collective refult; but on the other hand he is by no
means averfe to the benefits which are derived by the inflow of

wealthy and liberal people, who poffefs apparently all the bleffings of worldly life, with the exception of that health which alone makes the reft endurable.

Timber was at one time plentiful over a greater part of the ifle, but the vicinity of a great dockyard, which until almoft to-day was crying perpetually for wood, wood (the demand has now changed to one for iron) is not a guarantee for the fafety of forefts. Portfmouth has effectually thinned the timber of the ifle. What woods there are, apart from private grounds, are mere tenderlings ; their thinned fhrubberies, once oak and elm—the favourite woods of the navy—gave the ifle umbrageous fhadow and broken lines of fweeping landfcape. The oaks have long fince failed away over the oceans, and the elms are down, but the garden of England ftill remains true to the words Scott wrote of another fpot—

> " The roving fight
> Purfues its pleafing courfe o'er neighbouring hills
> Of many a different form and different hue ;
> Bright with ripe corn, or green with grafs,
> Or dark with clover's purple bloom ! "

It is only within the laft twenty years that the general belief has been cleared away that, before the Roman invafion, the Ifle of Wight, in common with all England, was inhabited by barbarians. Archæologifts are now beginning to difcover, that to accept abfolutely as truth in relation to the primitive race who peopled the Britifh ifles, all or any part of what has been faid by paft writers, is to err. Antiquarians are beginning to experience the good effects of the ufe of induction, and to difcover that a perfonal inveftigation of what remains of the early races, together with the indirect and unintended evidence offered by the one important writer upon this fubject, leads them to the conclufion that to infer the Briton was a

E

favage, even in the earlieft known times, is to be greatly
miftaken.

It is a matter of deeply-rooted tradition in Ireland, that the
country was once fo civilized that human life was at all times
fafe, and in all parts of the land; while the much difcuffed
round towers afford inevitable evidence of fomething like a
ftate of civilization at the time of their erection, becaufe a
large building is in itfelf evidence of an advanced, a fettled, and
a non-migratory life. Thence we infer, in reference to Wight,
that it was in the firft place peopled by civilized colonifts
from fouthern Europe, that thence this early people flowed
over the fouth of England, and fo on to the north. We
fubmit that when Cæfar arrived off the coaft of fouthern
England he met, not an army of barbarians, but forces of
difciplined men, forces no doubt inferior in military and civil
education to the Romans, but not therefore favages.

It goes for nothing that Cæfar calls the Britons barbarians.
It is a term which was equally applied to all people not within
the pale of the Roman civilization, and therefore it may be
accepted as of no more value than the fimilar term applied to
us by the Chinefe and Japanefe, and under precifely fimilar
circumftances, thofe of being beyond the boundaries of China
and Japan.

It is not to be expected that Cæfar, writing for Rome, will
allow that the Britifh did certainly drive back the Roman
vanguard, as the men compofing it leapt into the fhallow
water in which the galleys were anchored. But it appears to
us, quite ingenuoufly, he tells how his foldiers were confounded
by the novelty of the warfare oppofed to them. Now novelty is
not a characteriftic of favage warfare, while Cæfar had certainly
had experience of war with people of primitive and barbarian
character.

There can be fcarcely any doubt that the chariot-warfare difplayed by the Britifh, the marvellous ability with which the knight ran along the fhaft of the chariot and caft his javelin, did drive back the Romans, not by the favagery of the refiftance, but by its comparative evidences of art and civilization.

But the refiftance offered by the Britifh is not the only evidence we have that previoufly to the arrival of the Romans they were not wild men of the woods. Cæfar writes, telling how his foldiers were gathering corn from the fields, when the foraging party was fallen upon and flain. Now this aĉt takes place almoft immediately after the Roman landing, and therefore before the Romans had gained any opportunity of engrafting their own civilization upon the conquered people. Here then, we have the evidences of ftrategic war, and of comparative agriculture in favour of the theory that the people of the Britifh Ifles at the time of the Roman Conqueft were not in a ftate of mere barbarifm.

But there is another unqueftioned fhape of internal evidence of the early civilization of the Britifh Ifles, and one to which only a few years fince the Ifle of Wight, after the lapfe of almoft two thoufand years, contributed its atom of proof. We refer to the readinefs with which the Britons accepted the Roman rule—a readinefs which appears to us to be proof pofitive of one civilization at once rationally accepting another because a higher civilization.

In modern hiftory we know that conquered nations affimilate themfelves to the conquering, and therefore more civilized people, in exaĉt proportion to their own previous civilization. As an example, let us point to the conqueft of the Red Indian by the American, and the partial conqueft of Japan by the Englifhman. In the firft cafe the Indian is rapidly dying out, for the whites conquered no civilization. In the fecond, the

Japanefe, although only a partially conquered people, recognife
the value of that civilization which has thruft itfelf in amongft
them, and they are gradually accepting all that is good in
European thought and modern life.

We maintain that the early Britons were prepared to receive
Rome. The Roman remains, very few as they are, prove
that a very extended civilization, widening into the fhape of
cities upon fpots which are now mere wildernefles or fmall
villages, over a great extent of England did exift. Amongft
whom ? The Romans themfelves were no more colonifts
than are the French of to-day. They did not conquer to find
fpace for the people of their overgrown cities or provinces.
They conquered as a military people, with whom it was a
neceflity always to keep large ftanding citizen armies, which
had to be fpread over the whole of the empire, but which,
upon neceflity arifing, could be concentrated upon a given
fpot.

It could not be for the few thoufands of foldiers ftationed in
England that the vaft baths were built, the remains of which
are being found every year, and in the moft out-of-the-way
places. Then if thefe Roman baths were not for the conquerors, they exifted for the accommodation of the conquered,
and we therefore arrive at the conclufion that at once the Briton
accepted the Roman rule, and that the acceptation was a proof
of a comparatively anticipatory civilization.

No Roman remains having been found in the Ifle of Wight,
the conclufion was taken and maintained that the Roman power
had paffed over the ifle as valuelefs—unimportant ; when, by
accident in a garden in the very centre of the ifle, and suggeft-
ing a little metropolis even in thofe early days, the remains of
the teffelated floor of a Roman bath were found, a bath not fo
large as to fuggeft the idea that it was a public one, but

sufficiently extenfive to juftify the fuppofition that it muft have formed part of an eftablifhment of much importance.

The difcovery of that Roman bath in the garden of Carifbrook parifh parfonage, perhaps the very fite of a Roman temple, at once admitted the Ifle of Wight within the grandiofe if unknown hiftory of the Britifh Ifles under the Romans, a hiftory which has to be written, and which will effectually dispofe of the belief ftill generally held, (even by Macaulay,) with regard to early Britain, a conviction, it is to be feared, grounded for the moft part, as far as this generation goes, upon Goldfmith's ftupidly bad tranflation of Cæsar, by which in our youth we were taught to believe that the Briton wore his hair long, lived in caves, ate roots, and painted himfelf blue.

There have of courfe always been evidences throughout the ifland of the Celtic race. Villages and earth-works of very early date may ftill be traced around Gallibury, Newbarns and Rowborough. Nor is the ifle wanting in many fpecimens of thofe tumuli or mounds which form one of its great archæological puzzles. Thefe barrows are found in pofitive abundance at Brooke, Afton, Chillerton, and notably upon Mottifcomb Downs. At Brixton is to be found a huge cairn, while many of the laft refting-places of this early people, about whofe origin the learned difagree, but who probably came from the eaft by way of the Mediterranean and the Atlantic, are met with at Shalcombe, Bembridge, Wroxhall, St. Catherine's and Afhey.

Opened, thefe barrows are found to contain urns of baked clay (evidences affuredly of the application of fire to the dead), varying in size and fhape, and bronze celts, a fort of chifel, an implement proving beyond queftion that the owners were workers in metal, or at all events had dealings with artizans of that character.

Cæsar fpeaks of the Belgæ, a Celtic tribe, as landing upon

and taking poffeffion of the ifland (B.C. 85). But it may be
doubted whether Cæsar made this ftatement upon any ftronger
bafis than hearfay. It is far more rational to affume that the
ifland, in common with Britain, as the large army which refifted
Cæsar proved, had been peopled through many generations,
perchance centuries, and that the germs of civilization the early
fettlers brought with them had been foftered and advanced.

However, only a few years after the grand tragedy, culminating upon Calvary, had been played out, in A D., 43-45,
we know that Vefpafian brought the Ifle of Wight under the
light weight of the Roman yoke.

Some knowledge of the populous condition of Britain about
this time may be gained from the fact that Vefpafian engaged
in thirty battles, and reduced twenty towns before the Britons
of the fouthern provinces yielded once again to the Roman
power, liberty being fweet though bondage bring luxury.
Although therefore the Britifh accepted the Roman civilization, they again and again threw off the Latin bondage, until
through the paffage of a few generations, they became veritably
Roman in thought and life, fo that when the fierce hungry
Saxons poured down upon them they turned quite naturally for
help to imperial, yet trembling Rome herfelf.

By the year A.D. 240, the Britifh fubjection to Rome was
complete. By A D. 292, the firft Britifh fleet, anchored off the
Ifle of Wight, was ready to give battle in a bad caufe, for
Conftantius, the Roman Emperor, having been difpoffeffed of
Britain in the firft place by Caraufius, and afterwards by
Allectus, he equipped a powerful fleet, and failed from Gaul
for Britain. Upon this occafion the Britifh fleet failed, for a
mift completely hid the Roman galleys, and the legions were
landed along the Englifh coaft without oppofition.

And thefe particulars are all that we can find in the Roman

literature which refers to the little Ifle of Wight. But recent inveftigations, which are ftill in their infancy, have difcovered remains of Roman villas at Clatterford and Brightfone; the fquare outline of a Roman encampment near Bonchurch has been fwallowed by the fea within memory, and at one point of the ifland there are figns of an old Roman pottery. Let fome wife man found there another pottery, for your Roman potter never ufed other than good clay.

Near Ventnor, the birth of yefterday, which has no name in maps of the ifland of forty years ago, remains of Roman villas have been found; and now that the hunt for fuch remains is in full cry, we have little doubt not a year will pafs during which fomething fhall not have been added to the hiftory of Rome in the Ifle of Wight.

The Rev. James White, however, has carried the Latin theory very far. That gentleman says, " Many traces of Roman occupation are ftill to be feen in the neighbourhood of Ventnor. Wife men indeed (names not given), tell us that the dark hair and brilliant eyes of the natives of this diftrict are derived from a Roman anceftry." We rather fuppofe that, as in Wiltfhire, fo near Ventnor, the ancient Celtic characteriftics remain almoft utterly unchanged.

The Rev. E. Kell fays, " There are, befides, many roads called Streets, which if not always planned by the Romans were adopted by them. Thefe ftreets have, by their unufually large number in the ifland, the imprefs of extenfive Roman refidence. Thus, parts of the adopted Britifh tin road from north to fouth are called Rue Street, North Street, Chillerton Street, and Chale Street. On the weft there is Thorley Street and Street Place. On the eaft, Arreton Street, Bembridge Street, Haven Street, and Play Street; and again, Elderton Street and Whippingham Street from north to fouth in the Eaft Medina.

There is fome appearance of arrangement in the roads running from the north to the fouth, and of a reference to Carifbrook Caftle as a centre, in the ftreets from eaft to weft."

No, the ifland was not a barren wafte in the time of the brilliant Romans. They muft have found the ifle a northern paradife—a place, in part reminding them of Italy. They found out the genial Ventnor—fweeteft of names—and built their villas under the friendly protecting Undercliff. They built fortifications ; therefore, they founded towns, and here, as elfewhere, they obtained power. But in return they were tolerant, pleafant mafters, giving good leffons which bear their inherited fruit even to this day.

During the Roman occupation, that pompous four hundred years of the ifland's hiftory, which did its work and died, the Roman fhape of civilization was dying out and yielding to the Chriftian thought ; for we hold that Rome never morally declined, but has rifen over tyranny after tyranny, as fhe has always done, as fhe will always do, whatever the fhape of oppreffion. During thofe peaceful four hundred years the iflanders were protected upon the one condition of contributing their fair number of young men to the Roman army. Then Rome called her foldiers home, and a time of wretchednefs and defpair fwept over the land.

> " Too oft has this fair ifland been the fcene
> Of fierce contention, maffacre, and blood.
> The fword—great orphan-maker of the world !
> Borne by the Saxon and the rugged Dane,
> Laid wafte for centuries the peafant's cot,
> Filling each field and plain with heaps of dead,
> And making every verdant valley blufh
> A crimfon hue !"

By 520 all hope of peace was at an end. In that year Cerdic and Cynric (both Jutes) fell upon the Ifle of Wight, and flew all before them up to Carifbrook. The Roman inftruction had taught the iflanders how to defend themfelves, and they fought bravely ; but they were a docile people, who had been at peace through centuries, cultivating the fields, and making pottery for the Roman market, or oyfter fifh-ing for the great city on the Tiber. The Jutes were men who fought, as it were, after leaving burnt bridges and boats behind them. They were human birds of prey who knew that if they did not conquer they muft die—that there was no home behind them—that they muft hew out a prefent and a future with their fwords.

The Jutes were not driven out of the ifland.

A hundred years, and then approached the firft of thofe blood-thirfty crufades through which the Chriftian religion, fo mild in origin, has had to pafs. It is a miftake to fuppofe that the crufades were begun in the time of Peter the Hermit, in the eleventh century. They commenced almoft immediately after Conftantine had accepted and adopted Chriftianity—whether from policy, or conviction, or the force of fuperftition, we fhall never know.

The Ifle of Wight was one of the firft fpots to feel that Chriftianity could have a heavy hand. In 661, Wulfhere, king of Mercia, one of the very earlieft of the Saxon kings to fight confeffedly for the Chriftian faith, overthrew Cenwalt, or Kenwalt, king of the Weft Saxons, paffed through Weffex, now Hampfhire, and croffing over to the ifle, very quickly fubdued it, probably owing to the fact that the iflanders, ftill clinging to the hereditary remembrance of the comparatively benignant Roman fway, cared little to defend themfelves in favour of the reigning Jutic family ; and Ædelwald, king of the South Saxons, the land now called Suffex, having about this time accepted Chriftianity from the conqueror's hands, the victor gave him, as a baptifmal prefent, this fame Ifle of Wight,

F

under the exprefs condition that he converted the people of his
new province to the new religion. To this end the frefhly-
crowned fovereign was helped by one Eoppa, a propagandift.
But the people, who had moft readily yielded to a change in
the temporal government, clung defperately to the luxurious
and feductive religion which was then all that remained to them
of the old peaceful Roman dominion. .

But the early march of Chriftianity was inevitable, for it
was enforced by the fword. Through twenty years did the
iflanders hold their own, and then, fword in hand, "Cædwalla,
king of Weffex, aided by his brother Mul," fays Henry of
Huntingdon, "praifeworthy and gracious, terrible in power,
and excellent in perfon, beloved by all, and of a widefpread
favour, did fubdue the ifland, and caufe the iflanders to accept
cheerfully the faith."   . :

However, when we affume that the iflanders adhered to the
Latin mythology, and refufed to accept Chriftianity, we are
only ufing an affumption, which takes fhape from the belief
that the iflanders could not have remained four hundred years
under the Roman fway, without acquiring a tafte for the poetry
and beauty of the Latin faith, as compared with the horrors and
myfteries of their earlier beliefs.   .   ,   .

But moft authorities diftinctly maintain that the religion
conquered by the Chriftian was the Druidic faith. The chief
authority for this ftatement is the work of the venerable Bede,
who has given an account of the converfion of the ifland in very
quaint, charming phrafes.   But it muft not be forgotten that
Bede fimply compiled from Saxon chronicles, written unqueftionably by monks.   Nor are his ftatements borne out by any
internal evidence.   .

Now, as the Romans rarely interfered with the faith of any
people they conquered, it is poffible that the Druidic form of

worſhip may have prevailed. By the way, we have no doubt
the horrors of Druidiſm have been greatly exaggerated, though,
at the ſame time, undoubtedly human ſacrifices were made, as
they were conſummated, for that matter, probably in all the
religions preceding the Chriſtian. Yet at the ſame time the
attractions of the Latin mythology, through ſuch a ſtretch of
time as four hundred years, muſt have had enormous weight in
influencing the religious thought of the people. The venerable Bede ſays, "After that Cædwalla had conquered the
kingdom of the Geriſſi, he alſo ſubdued the Iſle of Wight,
A.D. 686, which up to that time had been abandoned to idol-
worſhip; and he ſought to exterminate the natives by a terrible
ſlaughter, and in their place to eſtabliſh his own followers.
And he bound himſelf by a vow, although not then regenerated
in Chriſt, that if he gained the iſland, a fourth part thereof,
and of the ſpoil, he would dedicate to God. This vow he
fulfilled by beſtowing it, for God's ſervice, upon Wilfred the
Biſhop, who was preſent with him. Now, the meaſurement
of the ſaid iſland, according to the English ſtandard, being
twelve hundred families, there was given unto the biſhop the
land of three hundred families; and the portion which he thus
received he intruſted to the care of a certain one of his clergy
Bernuin, his ſiſter's ſon; and he gave him a prieſt named
Hildila, that he might preach the word, and adminiſter the
waters of life to thoſe who ſhould deſire ſalvation.

"Now, I think it ſhould not be paſſed over in ſilence that,
amongſt the firſt-fruits of thoſe who were ſaved in that iſland
by belief, were two princely youths, the brothers of Arnald,
king of the iſland, who were crowned with the ſpecial grace of
God; inasmuch as when the iſland was menaced by the
enemy, they took to flight and croſſed over into the next
province of the Juti, and being conveyed to a place which is

called *Ad Lapidem* (Stone, or Stoneham), where it was thought they might be hidden from the fearch of the victorious monarch, were foully betrayed, and doomed by him to death. Whereupon a certain abbot and prieſt, named Cyniberct, who governed a monaſtery not far diſtant, at a place which is called *Hretford*, that is, *Redford* (Redbridge), went to the king, who was then concealed in that neighbourhood, that he might be healed of wounds received while fighting in the Iſle of Wight, and befought of him, that if it needs muſt be that the young princes ſhould die, at leaſt he might firſt be fuffered to adminiſter to them the ſacraments of the Chriſtian religion. To this the king confented; and the prieſt having taught them the word of truth, and waſhed them in the waters of falvation, rendered them ſure of admiſſion into the kingdom of heaven. And ſo, when the doomſman appeared, they gladly endured a temporal death, not doubting that thereby they would paſs to the eternal life of the foul. Thus it was, that after all the provinces of Britain had accepted Chriſtianity, the Iſle of Wight alfo received it, though, on account of the heavineſs of foreign domination, no one was appointed to the miniſtry thereof, nor to the biſhop's feat, until Danihel, now biſhop of the Eaſt Saxons."—*Bede, Ecc. Hiſtory*, iv. 16.

But the hiſtorian does not mention the fact that the converſion was not a very coloſſal achievement, for that Cædwalla had put all the wretched iſlanders to the ſword with the exception of three hundred families, who accepted the new faith as an exemption from death. Indeed, if Druidiſm greatly prevailed up to the feventh century, and then required for its deſtruction, in one of its laſt ſtrongholds, the almoſt total extermination of its adherents, it muſt have been poſſeſſed of fome principle of attraction totally unknown to us.

And now that long peaceful ſtretch of time, defignated

the Roman occupation, muft have paffed away even from the memory of the iflanders.   Never, from the time of their converfion to that faith of peace which in its early ages was fo utterly a faith of war—never from that date until comparatively recent years, were the iflanders free from invafion.   We have already feen how, only a few years fince, when the great queftion of fortifications was agitating England, it was at once determined that the Ifle of Wight muft be protected by a great military road—fuch a work that it has not been approached by any military achievement in the ifland fince the exodus of the Romans.

It may be faid that between 787 and 897, the ifland was never free from plunder and defolation.   The commercial profperity of the ifland muft long before thefe dates have wholly departed.

And now as the commencement of the feudal fyftem frequently threw king and feudal baron into oppofition—the fatal pofition of the Ifle of Wight told againft it.   An angry lord, fleeing from the fway of a king, took refuge in the ifland, and pillaged it; or fome half-outlawed Norman lord came over and laid it wafte.   Then, when either of thefe encumbrances was driven out by the legitimate king, there was more plunder, more bloodfhed—and no relief, except death, was to be found.

So many werethefeonflaughtsthattheyarenotevenchronicled; and it is not until we come to the year 1052, when William of Normandy was looking eagerly towards England, and Edward, entitled the Confeffor, was living that weak but pure life which obtained for him his diftinction, that we again find hiftorical mention of a mercilefs raid upon the Ifle of Wight. It is now Earl Godwin, who, being an exile and an outlaw, obtains a fleet from the Earl of Flanders, fwoops upon the poor little ifland, and ravages it of what remained worth the

taking away. The excufe for this murder and rapine was
grounded upon the allegation that the iflanders had been very
civil to the Normans, the great favourites of Edward the Confeffor, who had not himfelf behaved with fufficient civility to
the Earl Godwin.

It is a fufficient proof how utterly mercilefs were the acts of
the Danes upon the Ifle of Wight—how far apart from civilization—that there is not the fainteft evidence of their ftay upon
the ifland. They ravaged, laid wafte, created a wildernefs, but
could not colonize, and turned their backs upon the land, only to
return when the wretched inhabitants had once more, by peace
and induftry, made it produce wealth fufficient for the ftealing.

However, the knowledge of the arts and fciences taught by
the Romans could never have totally died out, for glafs was
manufactured by the iflanders, and ftone worked in the time of
the Saxons, from whom affuredly the Wighters learnt no fine
arts. As the time neared to that degenerate period, when
once again a Latinized race was to contend with the
Saxon people, who had to fome extent fupplanted the
original Britifh, and efpecially upon the eaftern and fouth-
eaftern fhores, the Ifle of Wight became a mere debateable
ground for the two parties—on the one hand that of Godwin,
who reprefented the effentially Saxon interefts; on the other,
of Edward the Confeffor and his Norman favourites. During
the laft few years of Edward's life Earl Godwin may be
faid to have been the king of the Ifle of Wight, for he became
paramount upon the ifland. And it is a fufficient proof of
the ineffaceable energy and activity of the iflanders that, not-
withftanding the inceffant ravages of their land and poffeffions
through four hundred years, fo far were they from defpair that
they, by their induftry, were able to provifion Godwin's fleet, and
even to afford men to make up the complement of his crews.

The Saxon Chronicle, which of courfe paints the acts of the Saxons in the brighteft colours, fays, in reference to this imminent period in the hiftory of England:—" In 1052, Godwin did, with his fons Sweyn and Harold, land upon the ifland, but they did not much evil, except that they feized pro.-vifions. But they drew unto them all the land-folk by the fea-coaft, and alfo up the country.". Other chronicles paint this incurfion in very different colours, albeit thofe of the Saxon Chronicle are fufficiently dark.

A few years, and the laft of the Saxon incurfions upon the ifland was effected. Once more Britain was under the control of a Latinized race, and from its influence, whether for good or bad, it was never again to be freed. .

Harold, the laft Saxon king—who had no more right to the throne, except the blind right of force, than the next fwineherd, and who was falfe to the true Saxon heir, Edgar Atheling, as he was unfaithful to the promifes made to William of Normandy—held high court in the ifle fome fhort time before the fatal ftrife at Senlac, afterwards called Battle; and the Saxon falling, William of Normandy reigned, and the Saxon fyftem of ravaging warfare was annihilated.

The character of the incurfions made into the ifland now changed. Fire and fword, in the hands of a Norman, William Fitz-Ofborne, once more fwept over the fcrap of land furrounded by the fea, but the policy of the Normans was not that of the Saxons. They did not lay wafte, with the full intention of "raifing" what they could, and of then departing. This incurfion was rather a policy of feudalifm, a policy by which a people was effectually fubdued and held in a fort of flavery, but which, at the fame time, though blackened by many fhameful conditions, did offer fomething like a bargain

to the people, and did certainly tend to bind a lord and his
fervitors into a fhape refembling that of a family.

Whether the dukes of Normandy were French or not,
whether the Normans were French or not, matters little.
However, if neither lords nor people were Gallic in blood, if
they were really Scandinavian, it is difficult to afcertain by
what means they came to ufe the Gallic language exclufively,
to the utter extinction of the Scandinavian form of fpeech.
Still more difficult is it to comprehend by what fuperhuman
means a people could throw off its language and take to
another. And, again, the queftion muft arife, why fhould a
people give itfelf the trouble—affuming them to have the
power—to change the language? And what end was purpofed
to be gained by fuch an unpatriotic determination? Let all
this be as it may, it is certain that the Norman conquerors
were the heritors of the Latin policy. They did not devaftate
to leave, they devaftated to conquer and remain.

Throughout the Saxon Chronicle, in its relation with the
ifland, we find no evidence that the Saxons benefited Wight
in any way whatever. But the hour in which we find Fitz-
Ofborne conquering the land, in that fame hour we find the
promife of benefit held out to the iflanders. The Norman
comes with fire and fword, with ,s terrible feudal rights, with
his confcioufnefs of being a king in *petto*. He carries with
him the power of life and death, of enforcing mightieft
obedience : the favage foreft and gamelaws follow in his
train, many of which ftill exift, the plague and worry of almoft
every country gentleman. But, exactly as the Norman paffed
the night at the battle of Haftings, in prayer, while the Saxon
fwept through the hours fhouting and drinking, fo this conqueror, Fitz-Ofborne, in fubduing the ifland, once more brings
in his wake, prayer, and the peace of prayer. He appropriates

the land to his own ufe and profit, he divides it amongſt his
more immediate followers, upon conditions of the military
attachment of themſelves and all upon their land to his own
perſon; but he founds a ſtately priory in the ſweet valley of
Cariſbrook, and ſoon ſeveral churches are riſing heavenwards.
Then follows a company of Ciſtercians.

In theſe days, when the miſſion of monks is fulfilled, and
the learning, of which they were the centres, has ſwept
onward upon the dominant wings of the printing preſs,
when we only look upon monkery from the miſerable point of
view it preſented at the time of the Reformation, when the
bad policy of the head of the Roman Church, through two hundred years and more, in forcing temporal power upon the
ſpiritual, had borne its fruit of corruption and wickedneſs—
in theſe days we are apt to look upon the whole monkiſh
ſyſtem as thoroughly rotten at all times and under all circumſtances.

No belief can be more utterly without foundation. Mon-
aſteries were the only practical ſchools of the middle ages;
and indeed, can it be more clearly proved that monks muſt
have been high-claſs men, than by ſignalling the fact that it was
a monk who led the Reformation. Luther was no layman, no
hard-headed citizen who had never uſed a breviary; on the
contrary, he was a monk who had crept into a monaſtery,
overwhelmed by the death of a friend ſtruck dead by lightning, as he and Luther were walking in a field—and had lived
twenty years a monk. Never did Luther condemn the
good work of a monk; he but condemned the monſtroſities of
a perverted religion.

The monks taught the Chriſtian world all it knew up to the
time of the invention of printing; then, as far as his ſcholaſtic
uſe went, there was an end of the monk. His firſt work was

G

the teaching of agriculture, and, therefore, it will be found that every monaſtery throughout England is planted in a fertile valley and by a running brook that can turn a water mill, which mills, for the greater part, ſtill remain. But it is not any the leſs a faَt, that the monks were the firſt millers, the firſt farmers, and, in all probability, the firſt cattle-dealers. To this day, monks, in various parts of the world, drive very excellent trades in various rare and unrivalled manufaَtures.

And ſo, though Fitz-Oſborne brought fire and ſword to the Iſle of Wight, he arrived alſo with many peaceful arts. Soon the ſweet bells were calling to prayer, ſoon the fields were being cultivated in new and proſperous ways, ſoon fruit was growing in the monaſtery gardens, and flowers, many of them ſince become wild in the fertile ſoil, began to charm the iſlanders.

For two hundred years from the date of the conqueſt the hiſtory of the iſland is one of peacefulneſs. Nay, it is ſaid it even became a refuge to that moſt miſerable of men, King John, who ſo very fortunately came to the throne of England; and we ſay very fortunately, becauſe the advent of a weak and therefore unjuſt king, is the opportunity of the people. Cer-tainly, John Sans-terre—and he died true to his early name—was chronically attraَted towards the conſtitution, exiſtence, and defenſive value of iſlands; and indeed, he granted to Jerſey, in order to ſave the Jerſeyites from yielding to the ſway of their powerful French neighbours, ſuch a remarkable charter that in all probability it was the form upon which was framed the great Charter whence England dates her national liberty.

If John really took refuge in the Iſle of Wight during his feeble fight with barons and pope, aſſuredly the inſulars kept well his royal ſecret.

But two hundred and a ſcore of years being paſt, the paternal

ferenity and peace of the iflanders—ferenity and peace bought at
the fole expenfe of feudal fidelity to the reigning lord of the
ifland—were fwept away: the iflanders were again to experience
thofe woes of ambitious contention which have always inevit-
ably fallen upon the people, whichever fide became victorious.

In 1293 Edward I. purchafed the feudal rights of the lord
of the ifle, and from that time the ifland loft its individuality
and became part of England. It was too near the main land
to refift. Could it have been further from the land, it might
have bargained, as did Jerfey, with King John. It might, in
common, have obtained all the advantages which both France
and England had to offer, and rejected all the difadvantages—a
pofition in which the Channel Republic remains and is likely
to remain. But Wight was figuratively only a stone's
throw from the main land, and its individuality was taken to
market and fold for £4,000, money of that day, equal in
value perhaps to £20,000 of to-day. The " perfon " who
fold the feudalities of the ifle, it must regretably be ftated, was
a lady, Ifabella de Fortibus, " Lady of Wight," to whom the
lordfhip had reverted only the year previous to the fale, by
the death of her brother, one Baldwin, fifth Earl of Devon-
fhire, and Lord of the Ifle of Wight.

It is faid this lady died on the very day upon which fhe completed the extraordinary contract which barred her family
from the rights of fovereignty; they muft have been of refpectable character, for it does not appear that they expreffed any
belief that their head had been poifoned as a very complete
way of fealing the compact. Nor does it appear that any
reafon was affigned for this ftrange and difloyal act on the part
of the lady.

The Hiftory of the Ifle

FROM THE DATE OF ITS ANNEXATION TO
THE ENGLISH THRONE.

———◆———

ROM the hour when Ifabella de Fortibus fold the Ifle to the Britifh Crown, to the prefent time, it has been governed, under the reigning houfe in England, by a line of Cuftodes or Wardens, who in early times really poffeffed fome power, but whofe authority gradually, almoft impercept- ibly dwindled, until even fo far back as the time of the Stuarts, the Wardenfhip was little more than an honorary appointment. In our days the Warden, now called the Governor, enjoys a comfortable finecure.

However, the family of Ifabella de Fortibus did not yield the point of poffeffion with feudal readinefs. The next heir, Hugh de Courtenay (and the Courtenays of to-day may well be proud of an anceftor who could deny the juftice of a Plan- tagenet of the fourteenth century), protefted before the body of barons againft this alienation, and he maintained that undue influence had been ufed to obtain the confent of the heirefs. A brave man, but rafh ; for what fubject, not being of the royal family, ever obtained a decided victory over a Plantagenet ? However, the court had the decency to allow the attempt on the part of the Courtenays to continue through a fcore of years, and then a decifion was gravely given in favour of the Crown.

In the time of Edward II., the ifle fell upon very evil times, for that deplorable king, exercifing his accuftomed idiocy—and the act was in itfelf fo imbecile as to be almoft an example of courage — gave the lordfhip of the ifle to Piers Gavefton, who accepted the office to honour it by being an abfentee. As the world knows, the barons having then held power through the great charter for a century, and being the defcendants of thofe who had conquered the weak John, finding a ftill weaker monarch in Edward II., fo effectually protefted againft Gavefton, that Wight was foon relieved from its new warden by the fummary procefs of affaffination: and now the king beftowed the lordfhip of the ifle upon the Earl of Chefter, afterwards Edward III., then about ten years of age.

By this time France was ftrong enough to be menacing towards England, and therefore the Ifle of Wight was a point which called for immenfe watchfulnefs. The governor, ex-pecting the ifle would be attacked by the French, was fufficiently forefeeing to order the building of twenty-nine beacons, and two watch towers, at equi-diftant points, fo that information of the anticipated invafion might, in the event of its attempt, at once be flafhed over the ifle. We are furthermore told that the valiant young prince made many wife regulations affecting both the clergy and the laity in reference to the provifion of men and arms.

As the fagacious prince forefaw, the French landed, and even reached Carifbrook, defpite the beacons and the precautions. But, the Caftle reached, the fortune of the day turned, and the French were not only thoroughly beaten, but driven back to their fhips with great lofs.

The ifland then had some breathing fpace until the next weak prince filled the throne, to wit, Richard II., when once again the French contemplated a raid upon England, with Wight for a ftarting-point.

But by this time intercommunication was in fomewhat an advanced condition, and the confequence refulted that in addition to the regular defence of the ifland, which confifted of nine companies of militia, which therefore made nine hundred men-at-arms, reinforcements had arrived, not only from Southampton, but even from London.

And it muft be admitted as a portion of the hiftory of the Ifle of Wight and the reft of England, that once again the French landed, and fo fuccefsfully, that they deftroyed, without impediment, the towns of Ryde, Yarmouth, and even New-port. However, the enemy was once again to fail before the walls of Carifbrook, which they very valiantly and perfiftently attacked.

It appears that the Englifh waited for the enemy at Carif-brook, abandoning the deftroyed towns with a readinefs it is quite impoffible to admire or excufe, and as upon the previous occafion, the invaders were driven back. But only after a vigorous fiege and great loffes ; and their final overthrow was, in a great meafure, due to the fuccefs of an ambufcade on the part of the iflanders, who laid in wait for the enemy on their way to furprife the Caftle at its weakeft point, and were fo fortunate in overcoming them, that the roadway in which the mafs of the French fell, is emphatically called to this day " Deadmen's Lane," while the mound of earth raifed over the flain, who were buried in a heap, gave a name to the hill, the ground of which received them—that of Noddies Hill, to this day called Node Hill, though we confefs we are at a lofs to comprehend the appropriatenefs of the title.

However, the defeat of the French before the caftle was not a final victory. They ftill remained mafters of the ifland, the Englifh continuing fhut up in the caftle, while the enemy were fufficiently powerful to levy a contribution amounting to one thoufand marks, as a bribe for the prefervation of the remaining towns. An oath was alfo demanded and obtained by the French, upon their quitting the ifland, that, fhould they return within twelve months, the iflanders fhould hold them to be their mafters.

The Gauls did not again show an appearance until the following century, when Henry V., plaguing France with his rafh and ambitious wars, the French very naturally retaliated. The Ifle of Wight, always a fufferer through tradition—poffibly as much as pofition—once again was harried by the French hofts.

But by this time England was beginning to fhape herfelf into a warlike power, and a prefence in the face of Europe, for hitherto fhe had been regarded as only a fecond-rate power compared with France, Spain, and Auftria, and much to the furprife of the Gauls, they were driven from the ifland, not only with great lofs, but after relinquifhing what little booty they had feized in the fhape of cattle.

And this was the firft occafion upon which the iflanders had depended rather on themfelves than their caftle, in the face of an incurfion into their garden ifland of an armed enemy.

A few years later the iflanders were able to parley with an invading French force, and to offer the enemy fair fighting terms; for the French landing, and demanding a ufual fubfidy in the name of Richard II., the iflanders replied that Richard was dead, and his fair queen Ifabella fent honourably back to France, there being no queftion of fubfidy ; yet, neverthelefs, if the French decided to try what they could do, they were at liberty to land to the laft man before the fighting commenced, and then take fix fair hours' reft and refrefhment, when, if they would, French and Englifh could have a fet-to.

Never was warlike offer fairer than this; but the French were uncivil enough to decline the fpirited invitation, bade the iflanders a courteous good-day, and once mcre failed fouthward.

Almoft another century-and-a-half then paffed before the French made another attempt on the little ifland. This event occurred in the reign of Henry VIII.; the iflanders were by that time becoming too well organifed to admit of much fuccefs, but they managed to land upon the ifland, and having feized all they could, and before the alarm had reached even Carifbrook, much lefs the main land, they beat a difcreet retreat.

The iflanders were now pleafed to furnifh themfelves with war machinery, which we find defcribed in the records of the ifland as " parochial artillery," a procefs which was effected by each parifh faithfully fubfcribing one piece of light brafs ordnance, to be held at the full difpofal of the French, and this inftrument was parochially kept either in the parifh church itfelf, or in a fmall building expreffly erected in its honour.

In thefe days we wonder at what appears to have been the ufeleffnefs of diftributing cannon, or, as the archives have it, ordnance, over the ifland after the manner of a diaper, when evidently the more rational way would have been to keep gunnery upon the coaft line. But it fhould not be forgotten

that every parifh was for itfelf, and it could be no great comfort
to Shalfleet if its ordnance helped to keep the French off
Yarmouth, but at the fame time drove their enemies farther up
the coaft, fo as to enable them to fwarm down from the Solent
upon the village of Shalfleet itfelf.

No doubt the origin of the furnifhing of this parochial
artillery was bafed on the long-handed-down memory of the
battle of Crécy, the fuccefs of which muft have been due, in
a confiderable degree, to the novel ufe of cannon. The
Englifh preftige in relation to artillery, aided in the firft place
by the myfterious Friar Bacon, certainly remained known to
the Englifh and feared by the French until a comparatively
recent period—that of Charles II. This king, being the paid
vaffal of Louis XIV., the confequent careleffnefs of the
Englifh Government, and the unequalled power of the French
king, enabled our neighbours, who were at the time perpetually
at war, temporarily to outftrip us. Perhaps it need not be faid
that fince the days of Charles II. we have recovered pofition
in the race of war and victory.

It is juft poffible that this provifion of artillery was one
of the very earlieft attempts made fyftematically to defend the
fouthern coaft of England. It is faid that towards the end of
the laft century, fome fixteen or eighteen of thefe parochial
protectors were ftill in exiftence, but in the reign of Victoria
no man knoweth of their whereabouts.

Pennant, in his " Journey from London to the Ifle of
Wight," fays that the neceffary refult of this introduction of
artilleiy was to make of many of the iflanders excellent
gunners. The parifhes were liberal, for they provided
carriages to the guns, and did not even expect the Government to pay for ammunition. Particular farms, or rather
farmers, were alfo charged with the duty of finding horfes to

H

drag thefe machines; though it muft be admitted the requirements were not great, feeing that the ordnance was of very
low calibre, fome pieces being only as high as fix-pounders,
while others fell to the infignificance of one-pounders.

The defenfive movement, having now very practically been
initiated (we have no doubt by the Worfley of that day), it
began to affume royal dimenfions, for Henry VIII. commanded
the erection of the building politely called Yarmouth Caftle,
which ftill ftands at the mouth of the Yar. The period of the
erection of this remarkable edifice is that of the alliance between
Henry VIII. and the Emperor Charles V. of Spain, a time when
Henry had not difcovered that his marriage with Katherine of
Arragon was inceftuous, an alliance which of courfe once more
threw England and France into oppofition. For Spain and
France were the great continental powers, and England gave
the fupremacy of power exactly as fhe declared for one or
the other.

In 1541-3, when the Spanifh alliance had long fince been
blown to the winds, when the Spanifh princefs was dead, Anne
Boleyn headlefs, Jane Seymour in the grave, Anne of Cleves
divorced, and Catherine Howard gone to the block—when
Henry had not only become the great tyrant of Europe, but was
breaking in health and the power of enjoyment—he vifited the
ifland, making one of thofe royal progreffes diftinguifhed by the
ruin of the gentry he honoured with his prefence. Henry was
the gueft of Richard Worfley, of Appuldurcombe, the then
captain of the ifland, who was equally honoured and overwhelmed by his royal vifitor. The King went to the ifland
oftenfibly to hawk, a fport he dearly loved while he could find
a horfe capable of carrying him.

This Richard Worfley, a good man and true, who had
readily fallen in with the fcheme of the Reformation, held his

own as captain of the ifland through the remaining years of Henry VIII. and the weak fhort reign of Edward VI., when upon the acceffion of Mary Tudor he was difmiffed in difgrace. It therefore need hardly be faid that when Elizabeth afcended the Englifh throne, Richard Worfley once more became a man of power, who willingly acquiefced in the Queen's direction " to care for the increafe of Harquebufey in the Ifland." The queen poffeffed, hereditarily perhaps from her father, fome love of hawking, and fhe made it a matter of fpecial truft to the governor, " that the hawks of Culver be not deftroyed." In Culver Cliffs, at that time, was a breed of hawks, the remains of which are ftill to be found in Wight.

And now the ifland obtained a comparative reft, until the Spanifh Armada threatened it, in common with the reft of the Britifh fea coaft. In our days we can have no conception of the enormous power Spain wielded in the fixteenth century; indeed, we may venture to affert that the Spanifh maritime fupremacy was far greater in that era, than now is, comparatively, our own in the nineteenth. For it muft be remembered that if we poffefs a leading navy, both France and Ruffia are not unprovided with the means of fea warfare. But in the time of Elizabeth, the Englifh marine was only budding into power. Indeed, it may be urged that the victory over what remained of the huge Armada after the great ftorm which almoft annihilated it was the origin of the fupremacy we enjoy.

The Spanifh was the one fleet in exiftence, and it muft not be forgotten that there was a large party in England which was ftill favourable to the oftenfible caufe for which the Armada was equipped—the affertion of Catholicifm.

Sir George Carey was captain of the Ifle of Wight at that momentous time, and there can be no doubt of his ftaunch

adherence to Elizabeth, for he was not only in favour at
court, but he was a fecond coufin of the Queen's—his father,
Lord Hudfon, having been Anne Boleyn's nephew.   Now
Wight rofe as one man, and put its forts, and parochial artillery,
and ftrong men in order.   Sir George himfelf appears to have
been a man of much forefight—doubtlefs he had thoroughly
at heart the dreary experience learnt by the iflanders through
many generations, that whenever England was threatened by
an enemy it was always the Ifle of Wight which was the firft
point to attract the invader.

The preparations appear to have been entered into with
remarkable readinefs by the Wighters.   But Sir George was not
popular with the gentry, and they conftrued thefe preparations
into covert attacks upon themfelves, and into implied doubts
of their fidelity.   Macaulay perfectly comprehended the
growth of fuch a feeling, for that hiftorian recognifes that there
remained much Catholic leaven in Britain, and which rofe and
demonftrated itfelf the moment Spain took active fteps to
oppofe the Proteftant religion in the United Kingdom, as fhe
had previoufly only too effectually oppofed it in the Nether-
lands.

Sir George Carey's manner was haughty and repellent.
Whether this mode of conducting himfelf was the refult of
natural bias, or a confequence of his near relationfhip to the
crown, it is quite beyond queftion that, while he created
averfion amongft the infular gentry, after events in hiftory
prove that this feeling could not have been the refult of a
general tendency to fympathife with the Spanifh attempt, but
of veritable perfonal diflike to the man himfelf.   The gentry
even went the length of drawing up a petition of remonftrance
to the Lords of the Council, by whom it was difmiffed
ignominioufly.

The Wight gentlemen however were not eafily thwarted, for upon intelligence of their defeat reaching them, they framed a forcible letter, which was addreffed to Sir Chriftopher Hatton, the then Lord Chancellor, he who had, faid fcandal, been helped to the woolfack by the elegance of his manner and the fprightlinefs of his carriage.

The gentry, at the fame time, in the moft loyal fashion forwarded a letter to Sir George himfelf, containing the information that Sir Chriftopher had been written to. Carey anfwered the communication with more logic than courtefy.

The hiftory of the difpute between Sir George Carey and the gentry of the ifle remains to be written, fhould the materials ever be found upon which fuch a work could be accomplifhed. But looking back upon the evidence of fact, we are compelled to come to the conclufion that Sir George was practically right, and the gentry practically wrong. This conclufion is confirmed by the fact, that it was Elizabeth's policy, whatever might be her perfonal defire or diflike, to keep the right man in the right place. Sir George remained mafter of Wight long after the Armada panic, if panic the fear of that powerful fleet can be termed—a certain proof that his captaincy was good. And, indeed, we hear of no more complaints levelled at him. But there is other evidence of his good rule, and fuch as will at once go ftraight to the heart and comprehenfion of every Englifhman. It is that given by Sir John Oglander, who in his memoirs offers good teftimony in favour of Carey. He wrote no later after Elizabeth's time than within the firft dozen years of James I.

"In Queen Elizabeth's time," fays Sir John, "money was as plenty in yeomen's purfes as now in the beft of the gentry ; and all the gentry full of money and out of debt. The market, full of commodityes, vending themfelves at moft high rates.

Prizes and men-of-war at the Cowes, which gave great
rates for our commodityes, and exchanged other good ones
with us. If you had anything to fell, you fhould not have
needed to have looked for a chapman, for you would not
almoft afk but have ; all things were exported and imported at
your heart's defire ; your tenants rich, and a bargain would not
ftand at any rate. The State was well ordered; we had in a
good manner wars with Spain and peace with France ; and
the Low Countrymen (Hollanders) were our fervants, not
our mafters. Then it was *infula fortunata*, now it is
infortunata."

Sir John, however, referves the grand proof of the fuccefs of
Carey's government, in connection with Elizabeth, as a final
argument.

"I have heard," fays Sir John, "and partly know it to be
true, that not only heretofore there was no lawyer or attorney
coming into owre ifland, but in Sir George Carey's time, an
attorney coming to fettle in the ifland, was by his command,
with a pound of candles hanging att his breech lighted, with
bells about his legs, hunted owte of the ifland ; infomuch as
owre anceftors lived here fo quietly and fecurely, being neither
troubled to London nor Winchefter, fo they feldom or never
went owte of the ifland ; infomuch as when they went to
London (thinking it an Eaft India voyage), they always made
their wills, fuppofing no trouble like to travaile.

"The Ifle of Wight, fince my memory, is infinitely
decayed ; for either it is by reafon of fo many attorneys that
hath of late made this their habitation, and fo by futes undone
the country (for I have known an attorney bring down after a
tearm *three hundred writts*, I have alfo known *twenty nifi prius*
of our country tried at our affizes, when as in the Queen's
time we had not *fix writts* in a yeare, nor *one nifi prius* in fix

yeares) or elfe, wanting the good bargains they were wont to buy from men-of-war, who alfo vended our commodityes at very high prices; and readie money was eafy to be had for all things. Now peace and law hath beggared us all, fo that within my memorie many of the gentlemen and almoft all the yeomanry are undone."

A few years later, about 1635, good old Fuller remarks that " the Ifle of Wight hath no monks, lawyers, nor foxes!" But then he wittily adds, that the faying " hath more of mirth than truth in it!" Captain Grofe obferves, at a later period, refpect-ing this felf-fame proverb, that " it was very improbable there fhould be a fertile, healthy, and pleafant fpot without monks— a rich place without lawyers—and a country abounding with lambs and poultry of every kind without foxes!"

But all thefe witticifms about lawyers and monks, like moft popular witticifms, are referable to a far earlier date than the feventeenth century.

Affuredly there is fufficient proof in the anecdote of the attorney to prove Sir George Carey's promptitude.

Sir John Oglander, on the contrary, appears in a weak pofition when he confounds the buftle of war and its over-demands, with the activity of peace and its over-fupplies. There can be little doubt that the Ifle of Wight grew in pro-fperity, in common with the reft of England, through that wonderful firft half of the feventeenth century, when the people, who had hereditarily refted content upon the laft national liberties accorded through the Reformation, were bracing themfelves together to reftrain the exceffive powers of the Stuart kings. During the time of the Plantagenets, the people had a fort of rough power to control the king by reafon of the fact that, to a certain degree, the foldier and the tax-payer were one and the fame man. But the advance of

civilifation, which has always tended to divide labour, was in
England, and in the feventeenth century, (as generally over the
face of Weftern Europe,) feparating the tiller of the foil from
the foldier.   Regular armies were drifting into fhape, and the
yeoman was taking alarm as he faw the gradual concretion of
a new power, which had no intereft in the State beyond the
unfelfifh one of nationality, and whofe fervice was devoted
rather to the princes than to the people.

At the commencement of the outbreak between Court and
Commons, Jerome, Earl of Portland, was Captain of the ifle.
It was his misfortune, as it was the miftake of many Cavaliers,
during that terrible fight, to pufh forward the diftinctive faults
of the Cavalier as his peculiar difpofitions, and fimply becaufe
thofe faults broadly protefted againft the aufterities held in
theory, if not always put into practice by the Puritans,
and upon which the oppofite party naturally fought to throw
ridicule.   Portland at once threw himfelf into the moft demonftrative form of the Cavalier, and fo evidently, that the
courtly Clarendon, mentioning the Earl in his hiftory, concedes
this much of blame, that he fpeaks of "his extraordinary
vivacity."

Thofe of the iflanders who held to the Puritan theory were
outraged by the Earl's public conduct, and ultimately he was
removed from the wardenfhip.   Clarendon, who is perhaps one
of the faireft and moft liberal of the Cavaliers who have written
concerning the firft parliamentary rebellion fays:—"The
Parliament threatened the Earl of Portland that they would
remove him from his charge and government of the Ifle of
Wight (which laft they did *de facto*, by committing him to
prifon without affigning a caufe), and to that purpofe, objected
to all the acts of good-fellowfhip, all the wafte of powder, and
all the wafte of wine in the drinking of healths, and other acts

of jollity, which ever he had been at, in his government, from the firſt hour of his entering upon it."

But while many of the iſlanders applauded the removal of the vivacious Earl, others led by the gentry, with the greater part of whom cavalierſhip was a poſitive neceſſity, petitioned for his reſtoration to his poſt. At the ſame time a declaration of adheſion to, and faith in the Parliament, was forwarded.

But party ſpirit was rapidly riſing far above compromiſe. Moſes Reed, Mayor of Newport, declared firmly in favour of the Parliament, and boldly aſſerted that Newport was not ſafe while the Caſtle of Cariſbrook, frowning above the town, remained in the poſſeſſion of Colonel Brett and the Counteſs of Portland. This Colonel had been appointed commandant of the garriſon by the King himſelf, while the Counteſs, calculating upon the intereſt ſtill ſhown in her huſband by thoſe of the iſlanders who had ſigned the petition for the reſtoration to his poſt as Captain of the iſle, had, inſtead of quitting Wight, taken refuge, together with her five children, in Cariſbrook ſtronghold. With the peereſs, in this military ſanctuary, were her huſband's brother and ſiſter.

And now the ſanguinary troubles of the iſle began. Wight was to play its part in the tragedy which ended in that final ghaſtly ſcene outſide Whitehall.

The Commons were antagoniſtic to any ſhape of royalty, and having iſſued orders to the captains of all ſhips lying in the Medina to give the mayor full aſſiſtance, Moſes Reed placed himſelf at the head of the Newport militia, and with his ſmall force of landſmen, aided by about four hundred marine rather than naval auxiliaries, abſolutely he marched upon the caſtle.

The events of that day afford a chapter in the hiſtory of the Iſle of Wight which is moſt ſtimulating. Warfare has

I

always brought out examples of the utmoſt female courage and heroiſm. The hiſtory of the Iſle of Wight is not deſtitute of a heroine. She was the ſelf-impriſoned Counteſs of Portland, who appears to have put the paſt-named Colonel Brett com-
• pletely in the ſhade.

The Mayor, ſummoning the caſtle to ſurrender, ſhe advanced to parley. The condition of ſtraits within the caſtle is a ſtriking example of the utter unfitneſs of Brett for the com-mand he held, and which he appears finally to have made illuſtrious by the reſignation of his poſition to a gueſt ; for the caſtle was proviſioned for only three days, while it was moſt inſufficiently garriſoned. No doubt ſuch a ſhort reſiſtance might have been offered by the garriſon as would have led to much loſs on the popular ſide, but defeat was inevitable. It was ſimply a queſtion of time.

The Counteſs advanced to the beſiegers with an undaunted courage, a burning fuſee in her hand, and demanded honourable terms as the baſis of ſurrender, declaring that if they were refuſed ſhe would defend the caſtle to the utmoſt, and would herſelf fire the firſt cannon.

There is no mention whatever made of the Colonel through-out theſe high proceedings. It is only charitable to ſuppoſe that he lay abed with a dire ſickneſs.

No doubt Moſes Reed was heartily glad to obtain poſſeſſion under any circumſtances which did not entail bloodſhed. A compromiſe was at once effected, and not only was the caſtle given up, but the Counteſs ſtipulated that ſhe ſhould remain within it until the Commons had been conſulted upon the queſtion of her ultimate diſpoſal. To be able to bring your enemy to terms, and then fearleſſly to truſt him, proves either that the limit of courage has been reached, or the borders of foolhardineſs croſſed.

In the caſtle the Counteſs remained a ſhort ſpace, when a parliamentary order arrived directing her expulſion from the iſland. And it is ſaid that the poor woman had to take refuge in the charity of a few friendly ſeamen for the means of completing the flight of herſelf and family. She was quite deſtitute of means. It is ſuch touches of humanity as theſe which make the hiſtory of misfortune not only endurable, but poſitively appetiſing.

The poſſeſſion of Cariſbrook was ſoon followed by the ſeizure of every fort in the iſle. The Commons followed up theſe acts by the advance to the poſt of governor of the Earl of Pembroke. This nobleman, neither unpopular on one ſide nor the other, was very cordially welcomed by gentry and yeomen upon his landing at Cowes.

And now there can be little doubt that Wight would have taken no further part in the rebellion had not the unfortunate Stuart, whoſe judgment always appears to have turned him upon the wrong path, been mad enough to ſeek refuge in the iſle—as virtual a ſelf-impriſonment as ever was accompliſhed, for a dozen coaſting veſſels could have effectively prevented any attempt at eſcape.

Jeſſe, in his remarkable "Court of the Stuarts," endeavours to ſhow that this movement on the part of the King was effected by the craft of Cromwell. But a rational inveſtigation leads one to the inevitable concluſion, that if Cromwell could ſo ſway the actions of Charles as to induce him to go into voluntary impriſonment, the Protector was abler than his beſt friend has endeavoured to prove him—the Stuart feebler than his worſt enemy has painted that King.

The tale of Charles's impriſonment in the iſland is better told in the hiſtory of Cariſbrook Caſtle, of which it forms part, than here.

With the feizure of Charles and his removal to Hurft Caftle, Carifbrook dies out of the hiftory of England, as from that time forth caftles for the moft part became either mere refidences or ruins. ´

From the date of the fall of Charles I., the wardens of Wight alighted upon peaceful times. William Sydenham was appointed in 1644, and after a reign of fixteen years the wardenfhip became once again ariftocratic in the perfon of a nobleman with a very plebeian name, Lord Culpepper. But iflanders are iflanders all the world over, and are unwilling to bear oppreffion, if oppofition will overcome it. The Lord was fo overbearing in manner, or at beft the infulars found him fo, that an appeal was made for his removal—a requeft Charles II., with characteriftic careleffnefs, completely overlooked. However, Culpepper fhowed himfelf fufficiently civil to refign. He was fucceeded by Admiral Sir Robert Holmes, who had beaten the Dutch at a time when to gain a victory over the Dutch was the neareft way to Englifh hearts. The iflanders welcomed this gallant gentleman heartily. He went into the ifland to make it the land of his adoption. There he remained through more than a quarter of a century, and there, at Yarmouth, the good gentleman lies buried. He died in 1692, and was followed by an unpopular nobleman. Indeed, the peerage does not at any time appear to have fucceeded in the wardenfhip. The new arrival was Lord Cutts, an appointee of William III. Being General of the Forces in Ireland, he was an abfentee after a very fhort refidence. The fact in no way enhances the fame of this warden that he became more popular after he left the ifland than when in it.

Dying in 1796, he was fucceeded by Charles, Marquis of Winchefter, afterwards Duke of Bolton. Of this nobleman the iflanders never appear to have had a chance of judging, for he was an abfentee, and in his time the firft appointment of a Lieutenant-Governor was made. The gentleman upon whom this honour was conferred was a Colonel Morgan, who received twenty fhillings a day.

And now the governorfhip of the ifland changed hands with remarkable rapidity. Between 1707 and 1745 there were eight appointments, moftly ariftocratic. The Marquis of Winchefter being removed, General Webb was forwarded in his place, to be fucceeded in five years by a diftinguifhed foldier and ftatefman, William, Lord Cadogan. He was followed by Charles, Duke of Bolton, fon of a former governor, and who was difmiffed from all his public offices in 1733. The warden-fhip appears now to have remained permanently in ariftocratic hands. John Vifcount Lymington refigned in 1742, to be fucceeded by the Duke of Bolton—once more in favour, and reftored, amongft other attentions, to the wardenfhip of the ifland. The Duke, however, foon refigned, to be fucceeded by another re-appointee, the Earl of Portfmouth.

He was fucceeded, in 1764, by Thomas, Lord Holmes, who was followed by a commoner, Hans Stanley. But by this time a change of adminiftration affected the wardenfhip of the ifland. Two years after the appointment, Stanley was removed, and then it reverted once more to the peerage and the Bolton dukedom, in the perfon of Harry, Duke of Bolton. Four years, and the Duke was pufhed on one fide in favour of Hans Stanley, whofe party was again in power, and who gave the new governor a life-grant. It lafted no longer than an adminiftration of that period; for, Stanley dying, the Duke of Bolton, once more, after an interval of two years, carried the day. And it will be remarked throughout thefe rapid changes how very little the comfort or requirements of the iflanders formed items of confideration in the act of

appointment. After feven years, the Duke dying, the
wardenfhip paffed into the hands of one, who, though not a
Duke of Bolton—being in fact the Right Honourable Thomas
Orde—attained afterwards to that title.

Lord Malmefbury was the firft governor of the prefent
century, and with him the wardenfhip ceafed. And what, it
may be afked, was the bafis of all thefe appointments and
re-appointments ? The anfwer is fimple enough. The place
was worth £1,500 annually, and there was nothing, or next to
nothing to do. A very fortunate thing for the iflanders it was
that the poft called for no work, or it would have been ftrangely
accomplifhed.

Through that entire century of frequent changes in the
governorfhip, there was only one appointment of a loyal and
patriotic character. It may be noted in a line—not many
before the prefent—that it was faid, " the Duke of Bolton
carried the day after an interval of two years." It was during
thofe two years the ifle was under the control of its one really
patriotic and local governor. For two years the warden was
the Right Honourable Sir Richard Worfley, whofe name is
well and honourably known in the ifland.

The Worfleys had, through many generations, the family
feat near Godfhill. This village is one of the moft picturefque
in the ifle, and one of the ancient parifhes that exifted before
the compilation of Domefday Book. It contains one of the fix
churches given by William Fitz-Ofborn to the Abbey of Lyra.
The church, which is of Saxon architecture, ftands on a fteep
hill.

A wild, yet not uncommon, tradition is told to account for
the elevated fituation of Godfhill Church. The foundation
was laid at the foot of the hill, and the men began to
build there; but the next morning, on returning to their

labours, they found that all the ſtones and other materials had been removed during the night, and placed at the top of the hill. They recommenced their work below, ſtill the next day all was gone. And this continued until they took the hint, built upon the ſpot indicated to them by inviſible hands, and by ſo doing added much to the beauty of the ſcene.

Its elevated ſituation, however, has more than once expoſed the church to danger. In January, 1778, it was ſtruck by

GODSHILL.

lightning, which ſo injured the old building, that a portion fell in the following year.

In its tower are five bells and a clock. It contains many curious monuments, and ſome modern ones to the memory of the Worſleys. It is a vicarage, in the gift of Queen's College, Oxford, and joined to the rectory of Niton.

Appuldurcombe, the home of thoſe worthies of the iſland,

the Worſleys, is uſually derived from the Britiſh *Y pul dur y cwm*—"the lake in the hollow"—but the correct etymology is evidently *Apuldre-combe*, the valley of apple-trees.

A comparatively old account of Appuldurcombe ſays :— "The manſion itſelf, which ſtands on the ſite of a very old manor-houſe, is comparatively modern, having been begun in 1710 by Sir Robert Worſley (who left it in a very incomplete ſtate), and finiſhed by his grandſon many years after. Here was written the hiſtory of the iſland, to which we have elſewhere referred. This book, which bears the name of Sir Richard, was in fact the production of three ſucceſſive generations of the Worſleys. It was commenced by Sir Robert, who died in 1747 ; continued by his ſon, Sir Thomas ; and finiſhed and publiſhed by his grandſon, Sir Richard, in 1781. The love of their native place, and the deſire of illuſtrating it, laudably deſcended from father to ſon.

"The houſe of Appuldurcombe contains a choice aſſemblage of beautiful objects of art and antiquity to intereſt the touriſt. There is a large collection of paintings, drawings, ſtatues, and baſſi-relievi. Some of the pictures, particularly the hiſtorical portraits, were in the old manor-houſe for many generations, and were preſented to the Worſleys by the princes and great perſonages they repreſent.

"The ſculptures and drawings were collected by Sir Richard, the laſt baronet, who, in the courſe of the years 1785-86 and '87, made an extenſive tour through Italy, Greece, Egypt, and Turkey, and took with him able artiſts, who made the drawings and views of the moſt intereſting places under his own inſpection."

The glory of the houſe has now departed ; yet, even in its denuded condition, it claims the touriſt's admiration, from the beauty of its extenſive grounds and the ſtatelineſs of the large

Corinthian pile, with its projecting wings, which crowns the head of the green and ample flope.

Wyndham faid of this place:—"It is fituated at fome diftance from the road, within the park, and, being built from the quarries of Portland, and unincumbered with adjoining offices, offers a magnificent object to the high road and to the hills above it, particularly when the rays of the fun are reflected from its beautiful ftone."

Long after him, Knight remarked:—"The park is very famous, and it deferves its celebrity. It is very extenfive for the ifland; the ground is confiderably diverfified, and there are noble views over the wide glades. Oak, elm, and beech-trees of ftately fize abound, and the plantations are well arranged. The park and the houfe are, in fhort, on a correfponding ftyle of grandeur."

To return to the hiftory of the wardens of the ifland. With the life of the Lord Malmefbury expired what of feparate exiftence from Hampfhire the ifle ftill poffeffed. It merged into the municipal fway of a more powerful neighbour, an example of that modern policy which tends to breadth of control as in an earlier age it was an admirable example of the feudal form of government which diftinguifhed its firft Norman mafters.

It became, what it remains, the garden ground, the plefaunce, the convalefcent hofpital of London and South-Eaftern England—a little fpot, which after having fuffered more for its fize than any other in England, during the wars between Church and State, and State and Commons, now finds its miffion to be the affuagement of fuffering and the endeavour to reftore that health which has been injured by anxiety and the unhealthinefs of town life. The Ifle of Wight is a little gem fet in the fouthern Englifh fea.

K

Ryde.

—◆—

HE approach to Ryde is perhaps the moſt delightful that the iſland affords—for Cowes appears broken, Brading is ſhut in, Yarmouth is round a corner, and Ventnor has no pier.

Riſing from the ſhore, the town looks as though ſpread to be looked at, while the framing of foliage on right and left is very picturefque. Away to the weſt one can ſee the towers of Oſborne, half neſtling in woods, while to the eaſt the ſhore ſhelves away towards Brading.

A long, broad, handſome pier is this of Ryde, together with a tramway, well-managed and well-appointed, but the ſeating accommodation on the pier itſelf is of a ſtrangely primitive kind, while the complicated financial arrangements at the turnſtile are calculated equally to ſtir up one's aſtoniſhment and arithmetic.

Ryde is the baſe line whence the touriſts iſſue to conquer a

knowledge of the beauties of the ifland—and indeed, by very
judicious management we may fweep over the whole of the
north, eaft, fouth, and centre of the ifland, and yet fleep every
night in Ryde itfelf—a rational proceeding, perhaps, when we
may be called fuddenly away, but one which is injudicious
when time is wholly one's own. There is nothing more
delightful than rifking accommodation, and experimenting upon
the fare and " wine of the country"—as Queen Mary's hufband,
Philip of Spain, called the huge goblet of beer offered him
when he landed in England, and which he fuppofed it was
imperative he fhould drink off.

It is an excitement to reft at a wonderfully difcovered little
rural inn—though certainly, in the Ifle of Wight, the inhabitants cannot be condemned on the fcore of village ale-houfes,
for they do not appear to exift to any extent.

The hotels at Ryde are not any worfe than at other
watering-places, while indeed, they are faid to be a little
more confiderate towards vifitors than elfewhere. Ryde, however, is a colony of lodging-houfes, and in the feafon it is one
that feldom needs to call for fettlers. In Auguft, when the
butterfly yachts fwarm to Ryde, it is, indeed, difficult to find a
place in which to lay the weary head. And yet, in fpite of this
wonderful popularity, of this influx of vifitors, even in Ryde
very primitive people are to be found. Not three years fince,
a benighted couple of tourifts, houfelefs, bedlefs, and forlorn,
were taken in by fome honeft people who knew nothing of
lodgers, and who having bedded and breakfafted them for a
week, did actually charge three fhillings for the accommodation, and fixpence a-piece for each meal.

Ryde has felt the bleffings of peace as thoroughly as any
part of the United Kingdom. Immediately after the downfall
of Napoleon, the Ifle of Wight—which, during the long wars

between France and England, never could be profperous in
confequence of its pofition, and the fuccefs which might
attend a landing—began to grow rapidly.   In 1801—for
we are going to weary our readers with a few, a very few
figures—the population was under a thoufand fouls.   In 1821,
half-a-dozen years after the fall of the great Corfican, it had
rifen to nearly three thoufand.   In this year of grace (1868) the
town owns to nearly ten thoufand inhabitants in two thoufand
houfes, exclufive of vifitors.

Of courfe Ryde has a fort of municipality, but it is not
burdened with a mayor.   The Board of Commiffioners confifts of twenty-feven members, who go out once a year.   Each
commiffioner muft be worth £700, or be rated at not lefs than
£20 per annum.

Thefe commiffioners lay out about £2,000 a year on the town,
while the poor rate, fome few years fince, produced £1,500.
Two or three more figures and we will leave them.   The
peace of the town is looked after by fix conftables and one
fergeant, all of whom are remarkable for wearing the moft
frightful hats ever invented.   Vifitors are days before they grow
accuftomed to this head-covering, which is worn by individuals
who apparently have a very eafy time of it ; for if the Ifle of
Wight in wild times has had to fuffer, and fuffer very feverely,
now that comparative peace has fallen upon Europe, the iflet
has its advantages—for your thieves, vagrants, gipfies, and
other nomads love not a fpot whence they can only efcape
by two or three gates.   No man can hide in Wight ; Charles
Stuart, amongft others, made that difcovery ; and to efcape
from the place a fugitive muft either hire a private boat, or
endeavour to fly by one of the gates—which are three—Ryde,
Cowes, and Yarmouth.   All men going to or from the ifland
pafs by one of thefe points.

The confequence is that the lower thieving and begging fraternity, not being able to tramp into the land after their ordinary fafhion, and the police keeping a very clofe watch upon the points of difembarkation, the ifle is remarkably free from the plague of mendicity. And thus it is that you may walk from one end to the other and not meet a beggar: a great improvement upon all Kent, which county, during Auguft, September, and October, owing to the hop-picking vifitors, and the begging traditions which have fwept down from the palmy days of Canterbury—then the metropolis of the Anglo-Roman Church—is fo offenfive, if not even dangerous, that ladies are virtually debarred from walking beyond the boundaries of the towns.

"Have you any gipfies in the ifle?" we afked, at Newport.

"Well, sir," was the anfwer, "gipfies have come, but fomehow they have gone away again, almoft as foon as they got here."

This is of courfe the cafe, although the Zingari muft know how much fine camping ground there is in the ifle. The gipfy is incapable of refting in a land in which he knows his foot is limited to a poor ftretch of under eight leagues. He muft be able to walk off acrofs two or three hundred miles, or he feels as though in a prifon. Again, the Zingari are certainly given to thieving, and, as we have faid, nature has aided the police fo much in Wight, that—— in a word, the gipfies are of a mind with the beggars and the thieves, and give the place a wide berth.

The police, therefore, have to confine their attention to occafional arrivals of the fwell-mob (who fet detection at defiance), and the fettlement of occafional difputes of flymen and boatmen with thofe of their tourift cuftomers who cannot fubmit to pay for the feafon without a little violent proteft.

From Ryde coaches pour out upon the ifland, although the rail, which is now open to Ventnor, has overtaken and overthrown many of thofe horfed machines.   It is alfo from Ryde that boats ftart for what may be called the circumnavigation or the ifland—a fix hours' voyage.

That libraries, news-rooms, and bazaars abound in Ryde may be taken for granted.   Nay, the town even boafts of a theatre, the ufual wretched, bankrupt, out-at-elbows, and difreputable temple one finds nine times out of ten at every feafide refort.   It was here that Edmund Kean and the people of Ryde had a difference.   It was a fomething in his domeftic arrangements which brought him into difcredit, and confounding the man and the actor, by fome means Edmund got hiffed, the refult being that the tragedian, who was playing Richard III., went the extreme length of intimating that his opinion of the people of Ryde was that they were donkeys.

No, the Theatre Royal Ryde is not a comfortable building. People will not go to it—in fact, people go out of town to efcape from theatres.   Poffibly it would be quite judicious conduct on the part of the inhabitants of fea-fide towns to buy up the theatres and fell them for rubbifh; fuch action would make the towns quite refpectable.

The true theatre of the Ifle of Wight is the theatre of nature.   What need of a canvas garden when every fquare yard of the ifland is a feries of leffons in botany ?   What need of a pafteboard caftle, when there is wonderful Carifbrook to wander over ?   The ifle is its own theatre, and laughs at that poor little rival perched on the hill, and pufhing forward its bald face and haggard walls like fome old coquette who will not underftand that fhe is *paffée*.

However, we muft not forget that here Mrs. Jordan, the celebrated actrefs of George IV.'s days, made her laft appearance in public—a great woman for fo fmall a ftage. She played on her way to France, feeking in that land, as many before her and fince, the health which had abandoned her in England. With Mrs. Jordan's final appearance the Ryde theatre drifted into its prefent condition, in which it is only too likely to remain.

The pier, the chief charm of Ryde, is the natural refult of the fhallownefs of the Ryde waters. Previous to its erection a fhort jetty was the only means of landing offered by Ryde to its vifitors, who, did they arrive at low water, had at leaft the charm of choice as to one of two ways of reaching the fhore, for at low tide the jetty was of no ufe. The option lay between going to fhore in a cart, drawn by a fteady old horfe, or taking a fedan (the more ariftocratic mode), borne by a couple of able-bodied amphibious bipeds. Each mode had its advantages and difadvantages. In the firft cafe you felt that you and your luggage would not get an impromptu bath; on the other hand the fedan was dignified and felect. But there was a great drawback in the fear that one or other of the marine runners might ftumble, when, if the patient did not plunge violently forward into the fea, it would be becaufe he obtained that refrefhment on his back.

The pier began to grow in 1813, but before it had reached its prefent ftretch, which is nearly half-a-mile, at the very ftart the conftruction engulfed 2,400 fhares at £50 a fhare— £120,000.

The look-out from the head of the pier is delightfully varied. In fhore are the reclining terraces of houfes, white being the prevailing colour, the ifland ftretching away on each fide in wooded hills, capped at one point by the towers of Ofborne, at another by the Nab Light. Away in front lies Spithead, generally with a frowning man-of-war motionlefs and gigantic in the mid-way. Beyond is Portfmouth Harbour, looking much like a Dutch town; and farther ftill the blue line of Hampfhire hills.

It was twenty years from the date of the completion of the pier before the efplanade was commenced (1856). However, modern engineers get through their work quickly, and the wall was foon completed. But it appears never to have become very popular, perhaps becaufe it is fo utterly wanting in fhade. However, it gave a facing to the lower portions of the town, and it remains of great ufe as an example of general improvement.

To the left of the pier—over this efplanade, and looking towards the town—is the duver, or dovor. It was once a ftretch of fand; it is now a colony of houfes, built for the greater part within the memory of fome fcarcely more than middle-aged. Many can prattle over their crockery mugs of beer of the ghaftly hiftory with which it is connected.

Here, upon this fpot, this dovor, were buried fcores upon fcores of thofe who died in the *Royal George*, when that gallant fhip went down. The veffel was outward bound, her complement on board, the decks crowded with vifitors, many of them women taking leave of the men.

Here is the tale of the *Royal George*.

Previous to failing, it was deemed neceffary to examine the fhip's bottom; and for that purpofe fhe was laid on her fide. This was done early in the morning of a fine day. The Admiral was writing in his cabin, and moft of the people were between decks, when about 3 o'clock, p.m., an unexpected fquall of wind threw her fo much on her broadfide that the flag at her maft-head dipped in the water; fhe then rolled over on the other fide, her yard arms touching the fea; after which fhe righted, and fank in nearly an upright pofition.

A victualling veffel was alongfide, which was fwallowed up in the whirlpool caufed by the finking of fo vaft a body. Other fmall craft in the vicinity were much endangered, but efcaped.

The fhip was crowded with people from the fhore, who were taking leave of their relatives and friends. It was eftimated that three hundred vifitors, including the wives and children of the failors, were on board. The crew amounted to nearly nine hundred. The boats of the fleet faved many who had been on deck ; but the admiral, with feveral officers, and the greater part of the men who were below, fank with the veffel. Only three hundred were refcued. It was impoffible to afcertain the exact number of fouls on board at the time of the cataftrophe, but it was calculated that nearly one thoufand individuals were hurried into eternity.

Admiral Kempenfeldt was nearly feventy years of age, and was widely lamented. He was confidered one of the firft amongft naval officers for courage, judgment, nautical fkill, and humanity.

The *Royal George* had had more flags hoifted in her than any other fhip in the navy. She had been the flag-fhip of our greateft commanders, and on the moft important occafions. She alfo carried heavier metal and taller mafts than any other veffel in the fervice.

The weather was fcarcely to be called frefh. No fufpicion of danger exifted. All that ever can be known is, that there muft have been fome bad feamanfhip fomewhere, that the fhip went over, and that the bufy naval neft was in a moment a feething mafs of human beings hopeleffly battling for life.

A few moments, and the pain of the fufferers paft, that of the furvivors began. The currents, combining with the prevalent winds, fwept many fcores of the bodies into the bay of

L

Ryde. The fea caft up her dead, and the Ryde people came down and buried them in heaps—in great heaps that marked the end of the tragedy. Readers will afk: "What, were thefe poor creatures buried like the bodies of animals, where they were found?" Yes. The prefent generation would be aftonifhed to hear at comparatively how recent a date the law in no way provided for the interment of the bodies of poor drowned mariners caft upon the inhofpitable fhore. When the *Royal Charter* broke up, great was the tendernefs difplayed by the minifter of the parifh upon part of whofe fhore the dead were caft, and Charles Dickens has immortalifed that Chriftian work. It was different at the time of the going down of the *Royal George*. The dead were caft upon Ryde beach, and buried where they were found.

Mrs. Robinfon (Perdita) in her "Memoirs" has a tale very fimilar to that of Ryde dovor. She herfelf being at Brighton, which was then a fafhionable watering-place, faw the body of a dead mariner lay upon the Brighton beach through two whole fummer days. It was nobody's bufinefs to bury the unknown, it lay with open eyes ftaring at the heartlefs world; and, finally, it was mainly by her exertions and expenditure that the remains of the poor mariner were laid in the ground.

And what became of the bones of the broad-chefted men who had manned the *Royal George*—of them and their belongings who had come to take leave of the lads who were never to furl fail again?

"Why, fir," fays the long-fhoreman, who is afked within found of the fummer waves, and over a white-and-blue mug of houfehold ale—"Why, I've feen great lumps of bones dug up when they were making them foundations, over and over again, when I was a boy."

So thus it is. The men of the rare *Royal George* going,

ftrong and healthy, out of port, to fweep the enemies of England
from the feas are cheered, and hearty wifhes go with them.
But the crew drowned, the dead thrown upon the fhore they oft
failed from to defend, they are put in the ground a yard away
from where the fea caft them up.   And when the land is wanted,
" great lumps of bones" are thrown up by the handy fpade.

The hiftory of the *Royal George* is taken up again, 1839.

In that year, Colonel C. W. Pafley, of the Royal Engineers,
was employed by the Government to remove the obftructions
which the ruins of this large fhip occafioned in the moft
eligible part of the anchorage at Spithead.

Colonel Pafley's plan was to blow the huge fhip to pieces
with gunpowder.   Cylinders of gunpowder were depofited by
divers under the more expofed parts of the wreck, and then
exploded by means of galvanic batteries.

Colonel Pafley commenced his operations in Auguft and
concluded them in November.   The quantity of powder
confumed during the various experiments was 12,940 lbs.
Two feries of explofions (in Auguft and in September) took
place, and Colonel Pafley ftates that altogether there were
recovered from the wreck: " Twelve guns, five gun-carriages,
one hundred beams and riders, or large fragments of them,
exclufive of other timbers, planks, and copper, befides the
cooking-place and boilers complete, the ftem, and great part of
the bows on each fide of it, the two capftans, part of the main-
maft, and all that remained of the foremaft of the *Royal
George.*"

The Town-hall of Ryde is rather a ufeful than an ornamental
architectural effort.   However, it coft £5,000.   Its right
wing is devoted to the ufe of an inftitute and lecture rooms,
its left wing to a market.   The Town-hall proper confifts of
two rooms, which can be thrown into one for feftive purpofes.

The great fact of Ryde being its yachting, the Yacht Club Houfe, weft of the pier, is an important building. Of courfe it has a fmall battery looking feaward, far more ufeful than Yarmouth Caftle ; while its interior, being built for men who are generally London club-men, is very handfome and effective. The foundation-ftone was laid by the Prince Confort, in March, 1846, a year after the eftablifhment of the Royal Victoria Yacht Club, which entering upon exiftence in May, 1845, at once obtained a guarantee of continuous good patronage and fuccefs by an Admiralty warrant permitting the Club to bear the St. George's enfign. The Club now numbers about eighty yachts, having an aggregate of nearly ten thoufand tons. The entrance fee is five guineas, a fimilar fum being the yearly fubfcription. It is to this Club that Ryde owes the preftige of its annual regatta, which attracts all Englifh yachtfmen who refpect themfelves, and many yachting foreigners, to Ryde in Auguft. The regatta is of courfe exclufive, and therefore a balance is judicioufly obtained by holding a few weeks later in the year a fecond regatta, efpecially for the encouragement of the Ryde boatmen. Thefe are good feamen, by the way, but their efforts to uphold a protective tariff certainly tends not to the increafe of their earnings. Boats lie idly toffing on the fhallow water which might be at work, pleafantly dotting the fcene, could but the ftubborn boatmen fit down and calculate on a penny flate the comparative advantages of having a fingle crown cuftomer, or ten two-fhilling patrons.

Ryde has ftriven to be perfect in many ways. It poffeffes an arcade, the Royal Victoria. The Ifle of Wight has alfo its Philofophical and Scientific Society, the head-quarters being at Ryde, which is reprefented by a very refpectable collection of the antiquities and natural hiftory of the ifland. However, it muft .be .admitted that the peculiarity of all mufeums not metropolitan—and even fome of thefe do not efcape—is to tend towards mildew, duft, and difarrangement, with ftartling rapidity. The Society numbers a hundred members. The Prince Confort, who was at all times more than willing to advance the interefts of the little ifle which the Queen made, and ftill makes, her home during the greater part of the year, was one of the moft influential members of the affociation.

Here is the report of the annual excurfion of this Society, for the year of grace 1868. " The annual excurfion took place on Wednefday (the 2nd of September). The members affembled at the Old Town-hall of the ancient borough of Newtown, formerly Francheville, at half-paft twelve, whence they proceeded to vifit the extenfive oyfter beds in the Clamerkin Lake, where, through the kindnefs of Sir John Simeon, Bart., the procefs of raifing oyfters was excellently explained by the chief overfeer. The party on its return to Newtown perambulated, under the direction of the Rev. E. Kell, F.S.A., the boundaries of the ancient town, which was of a rect-angular form, 500 yards long and 150 broad. The ftreets parallel to each other were Gold-ftreet and High-ftreet, inter-fected at right angles by Broad-ftreet, Church-ftreet, and Bowling-green-ftreet. The ftreet on the fouth was diftinctly marked by a hedge-row, but had fallen into entire difufe. The other ftreets are now either roads or green lanes. About twelve cottages are fprinkled over the fite of the ancient town. A plan of the town, which is girt on two of its fides by the Newtown Clamerkin Lake, was explained by Mr. Kell. The members then affembled at Swainftone, the beautiful feat of Sir John Simeon, and partook of a fubftantial lunch, after which Mr. Benjamin Barrow, of Ryde, the prefident of the fociety, propofed the healths of Sir John and Lady Simeon, with thanks for their hofpitable entertainment, which was moſt cordially proffered. Sir John Simeon, in reſponding, expreſſed in the courſe of his remarks his ſatisfaction at the propoſed eſtabliſhment of an Iſland Muſeum at Cariſbrook Caſtle. The company, about thirty, then adjourned to the capacious hall, where a paper was read by the Rev. E. Kell, on the Roman origin of Newtown. Sir John Simeon exhibited and explained various ancient charters of the borough, of Edward II., Queen Elizabeth, and other monarchs, granting ſpecial rights and privileges to Newtown. He ſhowed a beautiful map of the family eſtate executed in the time of Charles I., and other intereſting documents connected with the ancient borough. The exceeding fineneſs of the day contributed not a little to the enjoyment of this very ſucceſsful excurſion of the ſociety."

Ryde is exceptionally healthy, even for the glorious Iſle of Wight, which is the more remarkable becauſe in all probability the beach, from its flatneſs, is leſs healthy than that of any other ſea-ſide colony in the iſland. We have no doubt Dr. Farr would attribute this enviable condition of things to the purity of the water ſupply, a condition which it appears contributes far more to health than the removal of refuſe and the purity of the atmoſphere. The Ryde waterworks are at the foot of Aſhey Down, four miles from Ryde, the great plateau whoſe ſurface ſupplies the water demand. The municipal determination to obtain good water, a determination no doubt founded on the knowledge that the badneſs of the water has helped to ruin many a ſea-ſide place—Herne Bay for example, where the waſhing water has been often ſtrained through a towel before the conſcientious viſitor could waſh in it—was not ſtaggered by the expenſe. The commiſſioners appear to have foreſeen that a good water ſupply would prove a good inveſtment in the fulneſs of time. The anticipation has

been realifed. Thefe works, for fo fmall a town, coft a large
fum, £22,500—nearly fifty fhillings per head for all Ryde.
The refervoir is two hundred and fifty feet above low water
mark.

Ryde is plentifully provided with places of worfhip. There
are three Church of England chapelries in the town, for the
parifh church is ftill at Newchurch, where it ftood when Ryde
was reprefented by two or three fifhermen. Mr. Davenport
Adams, fpeaking of thefe in his voluminous guide-book to the
ifle, fays, "The oldeft of thefe chapels is St. Thomas's,"
whofe ufeful fteeple affords a confpicuous landmark, "the
uglieft is St. James's," while "the lateft and handfomeft is
the Church of the Holy Trinity."

The Romanifts have a very handfome chapel dedicated to
St. Mary, in the High Street. The choir is remarkably good
—indeed its choral fervices form an item in the attractions of
Ryde. Quite a fafhionable throng pours out at the completion
of a fummer afternoon's fervice.

In Doomfday Book, Ryde is called La Rye, or La Ruhe.
It was burnt down more than once, and was razed by the
French in the reign of Edward II. In later times it was
one of the centres of the watch and ward of the ifle, and
one of the three favoured ports to which all communication
with the main land was reftricted. It was only towards the clofe
of the laft century that the town began to look up. It was fome
years before this time, in 1753, that Fielding, then dying, refted
at Ryde, when leaving England for the laft time. "Between
the fea and the fhore," he gaily writes, "there was at low
water an impaffable gulf, if I may fo call it, of deep mud,
which could neither be traverfed by walking nor fwimming; fo
that, for one-half of the twenty-four hours, Ryde was inac-
ceffible by friend or foe. I was, therefore, rowed in a fmall

boat as near the fhore as poffible, and then taken up by two
failors, who waded with me through the mud in a chair, and
at laft placed me on dry land." Some time after Fielding's
death the wherries came in as far as they could, and were met
by a horfe and cart, which took out the paffengers and carried
them through the mud and water to the beach.

Fielding tells how he found only one butcher in the town,
" but he was a very good one, and killed all forts of meat in
feafon; beef two or three times a year, and mutton all the year
round."

" The fituation of the town," he exclaims, " is moft delightful, and is the moft pleafant fpot in the whole ifland. It
is true it wants the advantage of that beautiful river which
leads from Newport to Cowes; but the profpe&t here extending
to the fea, and taking in Portfmouth, Spithead, and St. Helen's,
would be more than a recompenfe for the lofs of the Thames
itfelf, even in the moft delightful parts of Berkfhire and Buck-
inghamfhire." Farther on he adds: "This pleafant village is
fituated on a gentle afcent from the water, whence it affords
that charming profpe&t I have above defcribed. Its foil is a
gravel, which, affociated with its declivity, preferves it always
fo dry, that immediately after the moft violent rain a fine lady
may walk without wetting her filken fhoes. The fertility of
the place is apparent from its extraordinary verdure, and it is fo
fhaded with large and flourifhing elms that its narrow lanes are
a natural grove or walk, which in the regularity of its planta-
tion vies with the power of art, and in its wanton exuberancy
greatly exceeds it."

The environs of Ryde are as paftoral as Goldfmith's deferted
village. Here is to be found no fublimity, no grandeur, but
fmiling meadow land—land looking lovely in the funlight,
wretched in the rain. The woody flopes dip to the inland valley,

while every hedge-row is alive with ftarry flowers. As for the
fine primrofes, we have already mentioned their fupremacy.
"This ifland ought to be called Primrofe Ifland, if the nation
of cowflips agree thereto," fays Keats. But fhall we confefs
that to our ears the ifland lacks the fong of birds? Whether
it is that the iflanders have, from a miftaken policy, deftroyed
them, or whether the once famous hawks of Culver thinned
its feathered fongfters, Wight is not remarkable for finging
birds. Keats, Shelley, and many others have written in profe
or fung in verfe of the ifland, but not one of the poets has
a word to fay of its birds—the land, the fea, the cliff, and
efpecially the flowers, having engaged their chief attention.
Sings Shelley:—

> " In a dell mid lawny hills,
> Which the wild fea-murmur fills,
> And the light and fmell divine
> Of all flowers that breathe and fhine."

Brading.

RADING is a market town, four miles from Ryde, and double that diſtance from Newport. The town may be deſcribed as one long ſtreet. The original grant ſtrictly enjoined that the weekly market day ſhould be Wedneſday, but by ſome means the market is now held on a Monday.

The town is governed by a ſenior and junior bailiff, choſen annually, a recorder, who holds office for life, and thirteen jurats. The common ſeal is encircled with the motto, "The Kyng's Towne of Bradynge." The earlieſt exiſting charter granted to Brading was engroſſed in the reign of Edward VI. It is, however, neceſſary to ſtate that this expreſſly refers to earlier charters.

Brading poſſeſſes an old Town Hall, over an old Market Houſe, neither of which is uſed. In the Market Houſe may be ſtill ſeen a pair of ſtocks, which, however, have not been in operation for a long time. In Brading are to be found ſome of

the very oldeft houfes in the ifle, fo old that they retain
evidences of the time when England was "merry England."
Dotting the exterior of feveral are to be feen the rings once
ufed upon feftival days to fupport the tapeftry decorations
to which our forefathers were fo partial. Another evidence
of the kind of fports and paftimes in which our anceftors
delighted takes the fhape of an iron ring in the ground,
marking the fpot where once upon a time bull-baiting
attracted the king's lieges. In a lane at the bottom of the hill
is the ruftic dwelling of Legh Richmond's celebrated "Young
Cottager," whofe fimple grave may be found in the fouth-eaft
corner of the old churchyard.

Brading lies at the bafe of the emerald-toned and lofty
Brading Down, and is furrounded by the woods of Nunwell.
The great feature of the town is the Haven. Brading Haven,
at high water, is an extenfive lake ; but at low water the mud
banks, and the crawling Yar in its midft, form by no means a
pleafant profpect. The haven covers more than 830 acres,
and therefore it need not be faid that the level being fo very
little below that of the neighbouring fertile land, the practical
farmers and land owners of the diftrict have always looked
with regret upon fo large a tract remaining a wafte expanfe
of mud. Many attempts have been made to reclaim it. So
early as the time of Edward I. Sir William Ruffel, of Yaverland, fnatched a little of the land from the grafp of the fea, and
the firft Yar Bridge was erected. In 1562 another plot of
land was recovered, and in 1594 a third. The chief attempt,
however, was made by brave Sir Hugh Myddleton—him to
whom we owe the New River, and the general healthinefs of
the North Diftrict of London. This hardy engineer was aided
by Sir Bevis Thelwell, who gave £2,000 for a grant Henry
Gibbs had obtained from James I. Under Sir Hugh's

direction, an embankment acrofs the narrow mouth of the harbour was commenced in the December of 1620, and the works were carried on vigoroufly and fuccefsfully for two years, by which time they were completed. The fertile land was now cultivated, farm-houfes were to be feen dotting the land thus refcued from the fea, and roads were made. But at the expiration of eight years (1630), the fea broke through the embankment and fwept away all. From that time up to the prefent, no engineer has been bold enough to undertake banking out the fea from Brading Harbour. But if the plough has not again been fet to work over Brading Haven, modern thought and ingenuity have within the laft few years difcovered a means of turning it to moft valuable account. The ordinary agricultural farming cannot be applied, but oyfter-farming pays more per acre than the former; and experience leads thofe who have been affociated in the enterprife to the conclufion, that in a few years oyfter-farming in Brading Haven will be a very profitable inveftment. So far, all that has been done has been but tentative, and large expenfes have been incurred; but at the laft meeting of the gentlemen interefted in this induftry, fufficient evidence was forthcoming to prove, that in a few years Brading Haven will be far more remunerative as an oyfter-farm than it could be made by any other means.

Thorne fpeaks very pleafantly of the queen's town of Brading :—" From the mouth of the harbour you fee a really noble lake, embayed between hills of moderate elevation, which are covered pretty thickly with trees, in many places down to the very edge of the water. Along the banks and on the fides of the hills are fcattered many neat houfes, and a church or two, and the head of the lake is furrounded by a lofty range of downs ; whilft the furface itfelf, of a deep azure hue, glitters with numerous glancing fails, and is alive with hundreds of filver-winged fea-gulls. To one who has not feen, or can forget, a lake among the mountains, this will, if feen under favourable afpeets, appear of almoft unfurpaffable beauty ; to every one it muft appear very beautiful. An hour or two fhould be devoted to a fail upon it. The views from the furface are very varied ; thofe looking northward derive much beauty from the way in which the fea, with its fhips, and the diftant fhore, mingle with the lake. The view from the head of the harbour is, efpecially at fun-fet, eminently picturefque and ftriking. Clofe by the mouth is the old tower of St. Helen's Church. The church itfelf has long been deftroyed ; but the tower has been ftrengthened, and made to ferve as a fea-mark."

The Corporation of Brading ftill pays an annual fine, or fee-farm rent, into the Exchequer, amounting to four marks— £2 13s. 4d. Their revenue is to a large extent derived from certain dues on fhops and trades, affeffed according to ancient charter.

Brading Church is fuppofed to have been erected foon after the Conqueft, but independently of its claims as an object of antiquity, it deferves notice from having been for many years the fcene of the paftoral labours of the late Rev. Legh Richmond. The admirers of that interefting author who vifit the ifland fhould procure his cheap and elegant little hand-book to the fcenery, defcribed in the "Annals of the Poor," entitled, "The Landfcape Beauties of the Ifle of Wight."

Brading Church is confidered the oldeft in the ifland. It is chiefly tranfitionary Norman in ftyle. It confifts of a chancel, nave, and fide aifles ; each with a fmall chapel at the end. The building exhibits fragments of architecture of almoft all the Gothic ftyles. The fmall chapel at the eaft end of the fouth aifle, beyond a fcreen, is the burial-place of

the Oglanders, thofe worthies of the ifle. The church is
dedicated to St. Mary, and it retained until lately, fovereignty
over the parifhes of Yaverland and Shanklin, which were
compelled to bury their dead here. The church is diftinguifhed
for its braffes, epitaphs, and weather-cock, which is a full-
tailed barn-door fowl.

It was to an epitaph in this churchyard of Brading that
Dr. Calcott, while on a vifit at St. John's, gave prominence, by
fetting it to mufic in the form of a glee, which has fince
become houfehold. The epitaph, on a certain Mrs. Berry,
whofe grave is near that of her hufband, is as follows :—

> " Forgive, bleft fhade, the tributary tear,
>   That mourns thy exit from a world like this ;
>   Forgive the wifh that would have kept thee here,
>   And ftay'd thy progrefs to the feats of blifs.
>
> " No more confined to grov'ling fcenes of night—
>   No more a tenant pent in mortal clay ;
>   Now fhould we rather hail thy glorious flight,
>   And trace thy journey to the realms of day."

There is alfo another epitaph to the hufband :—

> " It muft be fo—our father Adam's fall
>   And difobedience brought this lot on all.
>   All die in him, and hopelefs fhould we be,
>   Bleft Revelation, were it not for thee.
>   Hail, glorious Gofpel! heavenly light, whereby
>   We live in comfort and in comfort die ;
>   And view in that bright world beyond the tomb
>   A life of endlefs happinefs to come."

Neither copy of verfes is fufficiently poetic to juftify its popularity on its own merits. Of Mr. and Mrs. Berry nothing is
known beyond the fact that the hufband was an excifeman.

Thefe epitaphs are afcribed to the pen of the Rev. W. Gill,
once curate of Newchurch. All the evidence is uncertain
beyond the fact that the firft is a plagiarifm of Mrs. Steele's
lines on the death of the Rev. James Hervey.

A more touching epitaph is that by Legh Richmond, written upon Jane, the young cottager, whofe memory forms one of the paftoral chapters of the hiftory of Brading :—

> " Ye who the power of God delight to trace,
> And mark with joy each monument of grace,
> Tread lightly o'er this grave as ye explore
> The fhort and fimple annals of the poor.

> " A child repofes underneath this fod,
> A child to memory dear, and dear to God ;
> Rejoice, but fhed the fympathetic tear—
> Jane, the Young Cottager, lies buried here."

A far more charming and poetic effufion, however, is the following, infcribed on the tomb of an infant:—

> " This lovely bud, fo young, fo fair,
> Call'd hence by early doom ;
> Juft come to fhow how fweet a flower
> In Paradife would bloom ! "

The braffes at Brading are alfo worth attention. Near the communion-table is to be found a brafs, once inlaid with filver, reprefenting a knight, his feet guarded by two dogs. The infcription is as follows :—

" Hic iacet nobilis vir Johannes Cherowin armiger. dum vivebat. Connestabularius Castri de Porcestre. qui obiit . anno domini millesimo quadringes᷾ᵐᵒ quadrag° primo . die ultima mense Octobris . anima eius requiescat in pace. Amen."

" Here lies a noble man, Sir John Cherowin, in life, Governor of Porchefter Caftle, who died in the year of our Lord, 1441, on the laft day of October. May his foul reft in peace. Amen."

In the Oglander chapel are to be found altar-tombs to the memory of Sir William Oglander, and his fon Sir John Oglander, which charitable gentleman died in 1655. Their effigies are in wood. There is alfo a memorial of the death of Sir John's eldeft fon, a loyal cavalier, who breathed his laft in exile.

The Church of Brading, of courfe, has its grotefque afpeƈt. Here, for inftance, is an epitaph written in deep carneftnefs, but which muft excite a fmile :—

> " When fhe afflicted was full fore,
> Still with patience it fhe bore,
> And oft to the Lord did fay,
> The Lord have mercy on me, I pray ;
> And when her glafs was fully run,
> She clofed her eyes without a groan."

The regifter, which dates from 1547, contains this very fingular entry :—" *Burials*, Novemb. yᵉ 20th, 1677. Jowler (alias) John Knight, of Merton, whoe, rather than he would be charitable to himfelfe (when he was capacitated), liv'd like a miferable wretch on yᵉ publick charity. He liv'd in a p'petuall flavery through feare and fufpicion, and punifh'd both his back and belly to fill his purfe. He foe exceffively idolized his poore heap of muck yᵗ it was death to him to think of parting. He was allwaies foe afraid of want, or yᵗ he fhould dy as he had allwaies liv'd, a beggar, yᵗ he dar'd not ufe wh't he had for his oune wellbeing, but liv'd and died with his beloved bagg in his neareft embraces ; and at length, yᵗ he might pay his utmoft homage both by life and death to his greate god Mammon, he voluntarily facrificed himfelf, and even dyed to fave charges."

Yaverland is about a mile-and-a-half from Brading. Yaverland Church is fuppofed to have been erected in the twelfth or thirteenth century ; and it was here that Legh Richmond made his firft attempt to preach extempore, and completely failed ; though he was afterwards celebrated for the power and eloquence of his extemporaneous difcourfes. This interefting fpot is graphically defcribed by Mr. Richmond, in " The Dairyman's Daughter." It is pleafantly fituated on a rifing bank at the foot of a bold chalk hill, and, being furrounded by trees, has a rural and retired appearance. Clofe to the church-

yard ſtands a large and ancient manſion, which was formerly
the reſidence of an opulent and a titled family, which has long
been appropriated to the uſe of the eſtate as a farm-houſe.
It ſtill retains conſiderable traces of ancient grandeur, and gives
a pleaſing character to the ſpot of ground on which the church
ſtands. In every direction, the roads that lead to this edifice
poſſeſs diſtinct and intereſting features. One of them aſcends
between ſeveral rural cottages from the ſea-ſhore, which
adjoins the lower part of the adjacent hill, and another leads to
the church by a gently riſing approach between high banks
covered with trees, buſhes, ivy, hedge-plants, and wild flowers."

Bembridge Down ſhould alſo be viſited when the touriſt is
at Brading. It caps Culver Cliffs, whence perhaps, the iſland
is ſeen at its beſt. An author, who, when writing of the iſle,
wrote with a love for every nook and hill it poſſeſſes, ſays :—
" At the Weſt end of the Culver Cliffs, and thirty feet
below their ſummit, is ' The Hermit's Hole;' a cavern which
penetrates about twenty feet into the rock. There is a path
leading to it, but ſo ſteep, rugged, and dangerous, that only the
moſt ventureſome would attempt to deſcend. Nor is there anything in the cavern to compenſate for the danger and difficulty
incurred in reaching it. Theſe cliffs are much reſorted to by
gulls and pigeons. From the latter they received their name,
culppe being the Saxon word for pigeon."

Nor ſhould the touriſt forget to viſit Aſhey Down, one of
the higheſt points in the iſland. No words better than Legh
Richmond's can deſcribe the view from this elevated poſition.
He ſays :—" Southward the view is terminated by a long range
of hills (Shanklin, Wroxall, and Appuldurcombe) at about ſix
miles diſtant. They meet to the weſtward another chain of
hills, of which the one whereon I ſit forms a link, and the
whole together nearly encompaſs a rich and fruitful valley

filled with corn-fields and paftures. Through this vale winds
a fmall ftream for many miles; here and there leffer eminences
arife in the valley, fome covered with wood, others with corn
and grafs, and a few with heath and fern—one of thefe hills is
diftinguifhed by a church (New Church) at the top, prefenting
a ftriking figure in the landfcape. Villages, churches, country
feats, farm-houfes, and cottages are fcattered over part of the
fouthern valley. In this direction alfo appears an ancient
manfion (Kingfton) embellifhed with woods, groves, and
gardens. Southward is a broad expanfe of ocean, bounded
only by the horizon. More to the eaft, in continuation of the
chain of hills on which I am fitting (Afhey), rife two downs—
Brading and Yaverland hills—one beyond the other. Both are
covered with fheep, and the fea is juft vifible over the fartheft
hill as a terminating boundary. At this point are feen fhips,
fome of which are failing, and others laying at anchor. Weft-
ward the hills follow each other, forming feveral intermediate
and partial valleys, in undulations like the waves of the fea,
and bending to the fouth complete the boundary of the larger
valley I have defcribed, to the fouthward of the hill on which
I fit. One hill alone, St. Catherine's, the higheft in the ifland,
and about ten miles to the fouth-weftward, is enveloped in a
cloud which juft permits a dim and hazy fight of a fignal-poft,
a light-houfe, and an ancient chantry on its fummit."

Quarr Abbey.

—◦◦◦—

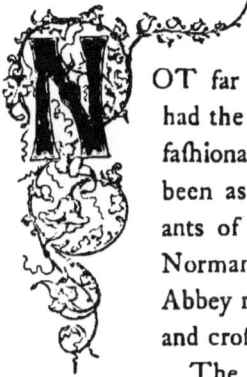

NOT far from Ryde is Quarr Abbey, which once had the diftinction, in its palmy days, of being fashionable—fashion in monaftic life having been as powerful as elfewhere. The defcendants of the trees which fhadowed the Abbey in Norman times ftill fill in what remains of the Abbey ruins, and make it full of fweet fhadows and crofs-lights.

The Abbey was one of the earlieft of which England could boaft, and owed its exiftence to the benefi-cence and piety of a lord of the ifle, Baldwin de Redvers. The building was ready for peopling in 1132-3, and foon a poffe of Benedictine monks from Savigni, in Normandy, took poffeffion. The Abbey was dedicated to the Virgin, perhaps owing to its eftablifhment being fo near the fea. And this dedication it was, which probably led to the more familiar title beftowed by the monks upon the Abbey—that of "La Fille de Savigni."

The fafhion of this Benedictine abbey was foon quite fettled. It became the mode for the knights and gentlemen of

the ifland generally, to patronife the eftablifhment, while it was
part of the very duty of the lord of the ifle to be its foftering
friend.   The monaftic fyftem was not averfe to the acquifition
of lands, and Quarr Abbey foon grew rich, and poffeffed eftates
at Shalfleet, Chale, Shorwell (one of the moft fertile bits in the
ifle), Compton, and Luccombe.   At many other points the
monks held land, while at Binftead itfelf, a large piece of the
parifh was attached to the Abbey.   No doubt the charity
beftowed by Quarr was equal to the demand made upon it.
Nobody has ever doubted the liberal-handednefs of the Abbeys
in dealing with the poor, nor muft it be forgotten that thefe
eftates were wrefted from the fears or liberality of the rich
Norman conquerors who had received their lands through
William I.

    In 1340 the Abbey was ftrongly fortified againft the attacks
of the French, and the walls around it pierced with loopholes.
A portcullis, erected where a door or fanctuary fhould have
ftood, annihilated all the peaceful religious afpect which muft
have been the charm of a monaftery, as it was the end of its
eftablifhment.

    And exactly as the temporal power of the abbots of Quarr
fhut out its fpiritual ftrength, fo riches and vanity got into the
very graves of the patrons of the Abbey, who elected to be
buried within its military walls.   The fimple placing of the
dead body of the monk in the fquare of ground furrounded by
the cloifters, was a habitude at Quarr which faded with its
poverty.   When William de Vernon came to be buried here,
it was found that he had left the equivalent of nearly five
thoufand pounds fterling of the money of to-day to buy him a
tomb.

    By this time the abbot of Quarr was the equal in power
with the lord of the ifle.   But retribution was hovering over

the Abbey as over every monaſtic eſtabliſhment in England. The rats had undermined their own dwelling-places. Almoſt the laſt magnificence of Quarr was the reception and interment, in 1507, of the remains of Lady Cicely, a daughter of Edward IV. By the commencement of the ſixteenth century, riches and faſhion had hopeleſſly perverted Quarr Abbey from all its original purpoſes. Nay, we hear little even of its charity—a partial compenſation which the monks have always been ready to offer. Sixteen abbots had Quarr, from its riſe to its fall. This gives an average to the reign of each abbot of nearly a quarter of a century, but Abbot Walter, elected in 1323, found the abbotry ſo good that he held it no leſs than fifty-five years.

When the ſhadow of the Reformation was falling upon Quarr, its rent-roll was equal to £2,000 a year of our money. By this time the power of the pen had been directed againſt Quarr. Lambard very early in the ſixteenth century had caſt a ſhaft at it. "Although," he ſays, " Paulus Jovius wrote that the inhabitants of this iſland be wont to boaſt merely that they neyther had amongſt them monks, lawyers, wolves, nor foxes, yet I find them all, ſave one (the lawyers), in one monaſtery, called Quarr, valued at 134 pounds of yearly revenue, and founded in the year 1132, after the order of Savigniac in France."

Came Henry VIII., and down went abbey, abbot, and monks; the building was given up to decay, the inhabitants turned out to find bread as beſt they might. Fortunately the men of Quarr were men of family, and therefore, in all proba-bility, the ejected monks did not die in the bye-ways as many religioniſts did, abſolutely of ſtarvation.

Commerce ſwept over quiet old Quarr. Two wealthy merchants, brothers, named Mills, called the place theirs, and

did what they liked with their own. What they liked was
to turn its refectory into a barn, its chapel into a ftable, and fo
was an end of the mighty Abbey of Quarr. A bit of wall, a
few windows, and a couple of doorways are, all that is left of
an inftitution which was eftablifhed in charity and died in
luxury.

In 1857 a road was being made clofe by the few ftones
which may be called the Abbey ruins, when the men found
an impediment which—but let us quote the paragraph that
appeared in the *Ifle of Wight Obferver*:—" Three fmall ftone
boxes or chefts, each cheft being about two feet in length and
one foot wide, were difcovered. They were placed fide by
fide,—two of them nearly clofe together, and the third a foot
or two to the fouth. Upon removing the heavy ftones of which
the lids were compofed, three human fkeletons in a good ftate
of prefervation were found. The leg and arm bones were on
either fide, the ribs and fmall bones in the centre, and the fkulls
at the weftern end, the latter being in all three cafes turned
upfide down. It was evident thefe remains had been removed
at fome time or other from the place of their original burial,
and that they were of perfons of diftinction was beyond doubt,
or fuch care would not have been beftowed upon them."

And now antiquarians had a chance. The bones were found
to be (1) thofe of an aged man, (2) of an aged woman, and (3)
of a ftalwart man of forty years. Is there any probability in
the happy fuggeftion that thefe were the remains of Baldwin de
Redvers, his fair lady, and their fon? It may be fo. One can
imagine that in the courfe of a century or two, the walls of the
Abbey failing near the founder's grave, the mafons were fet to
work, the crumbling bones of the founder, his dame, and their
fon were reverently collected, put into ftone boxes, and carried
near the chancel for burial.

A little legend and fuperftition hangs about Quarr, by the way. Fiom what ruined abbey is fuperftition wholly abfent? The tales told of Quarr feem to have an origin fimilar to the treafure myths of Bretagne, and may have come to England in the wake of the Normans, the neighbours when at home, of thofe people of Brittany, who to this day hope, almoft to a man, to become rich by the difcovery of hidden treafure. At Quarr this treafure, according to one tradition, takes the fhape of a fubterranean paffage, clofed by a golden gate; while in the other it is a golden coffin, which contains the body of Eleanor of Guienne, confort of Henry II., who was imprifoned here, and tradition fays, was buried in a wood fouth of the Abbey, and which is ftill protected from difcovery by magical fpells. What remains of this wood is to this day called Eleanor Grove.

Eaſt and Weſt Cowes.

———◇———

OWES began on the weſt, and taking in the eaſt, anciently called Shamblord, gave its name to the new town, and thenceforth the colony of houſes was divided into Weſt and Eaſt Cowes by the river Medina, which, in its relation to the town, well deſerves its name.

An author writing in 1808 ſays :—" This town, which is pretty large and populous, ſtands on the declivity of a hill on the weſt ſide of the river Medina, where it empties itſelf into the ſea. Hence its eaſy acceſs either from Portſmouth or Southampton. The lower parts of the town are narrow, irregular, and crowded. Here is a conſiderable trade carried on in every kind of pro- viſion, ſo that veſſels may ſupply themſelves with eaſe when deſtined to the remoteſt climes. The elevated parts of the town are delightful, boaſting purity of air, and all the charms of a variegated proſpe¢t. Not only gentlemen of the navy are partial to the ſpot, but many of the nobility and gentry reſide here during the ſummer ſeaſon."

The author goes on further triumphantly to ſtate that to
ſuch a pitch of civilization has Cowes reached, that a veſſel
can be had to take a traveller to Portſmouth for ten ſhillings,
a ſum which will now carry him to London, and in very little
more time than it then required to reach Portſmouth.

Cowes, like Ryde, ſuddenly roſe into favour, as inland
baths went out of faſhion, and the ſea-ſide was declared by the
faculty to be the moſt curative ſpot for the invalid. In ten

COWES.
(*From a Painting, by permiſſion of* Meſſrs. Bʀᴏᴡɴ & Wʜᴇᴇʟᴇʀ.)

recent years Cowes increaſed its population by one fourth. It
has no independent municipal exiſtence, but is included in
the borough of Newport. It has however, a local board,
whoſe members are elected by the ratepayers.

Cowes Harbour is the eſtuary of the Medina (here half a
mile acroſs), combining with the Solent Sea. Commodious,
admirably ſheltered, and capable of admitting veſſels of heavy

o

tonnage, its importance was very foon recognifed. Indeed, Cowes is the one point on the ifland which has anything like the appearance of a ferious maritime exiftence. The cuftoms now levied annually in this port amount to nearly £4,000.

Weft Cowes Caftle was one of the round forts built by Henry VIII., after his rupture with Spain, and when the threat of a Spanifh invafion, which was only attempted in the reign of his daughter Elizabeth, gave fome uneafinefs to the country.

Like moft other caftles built for the defence of a diftrict, it ultimately came to be a ftate prifon, and in the time of Cromwell this was the only ufe to which the building was applied. Here was confined Davenant, the playwright, the firft man to introduce opera into England. After the reftoration, Weft Cowes Caftle, in common with the other ftrongholds of the ifland, became valuelefs. In 1781 the "Caftle" garrifon confifted of a captain at ten fhillings a day, and half-a-dozen gunners. Gradually the caftle fell into difufe. But in our time it has been turned to account; for in 1856-7 it was fold to the Royal Yacht Club, who at once fet to work and made it for the firft time during its exiftence perfectly charming.

The chief dockyard and fhipbuilding eftablifhment is that of the Meffrs. White, whofe fame is world-wide, and who have built for every civilifed navy in the world. The fwifteft yachts upon the feas have been launched from their yards, where more than four hundred men are employed throughout the year.

With yachts and feamen fwarming at Cowes, it need not be faid that the ftreets, narrow and hilly, partake to a large extent of that oil-fkin and fhip-upon-fhore character which is common to all fuch localities. However, the outfkirts reached, many open and pleafant roads at once greet the eyes.

To the Royal Yacht Club Cowes owes very much of its

profperity.   At its foundation, in 1812, the Club confifted
of 42 members.   Here is its condition in 1840:—"There
are now 157 members, viz., 3 dukes, 3 marqueffes, 12 earls,
3 vifcounts, 7 lords, 18 baronets, 7 honorables, 14 M.P.'s,
1 lieutenant-general, 6 colonels, 1 major, 5 poft captains,
and 77 efquires—and 102 yachts of different fizes, from
30 tons to 451 tons; total tonnage, 9,632, employing
upwards of 1,300 feamen, befide fhipwrights, joiners, fail-
makers, &c.

  "Any gentleman, being the *bonâ fide* owner of a Britifh
yacht of 30 tons, or upwards, is eligible to become a member:
there are four balloting days in the year, viz., on the fecond
Saturday in May, at the Thatched Houfe Tavern, London;
on the fecond Friday in July, on the fecond Friday in Auguft,
and on the firft Friday in September; the three laft at the
R.Y.C. Houfe, Cowes.

  "There are 502 honorary members, confifting principally of
admirals and captains in the royal navy.

  "The members pay an entrance fee of £15, and a fubfcription of £8 annually.   The honorary members pay no fubfcription, except they ufe the houfe and reading room, and then £1
per year: they are allowed to board and lodge in the houfe, the
fame as the members, except between the 15th and 25th of
Auguft.   Each member can introduce a friend to the houfe for
fourteen days; and if longer, the member muft renew his
friend's name in the vifitor's book at the end of each term;
the member's friend fo introduced has the ufe of the library,
reading room, and houfe, gratis."

  Since 1840 the importance of the Club has wonderfully augmented.   It now includes nearly 200 members, poffeffing
feven fcore yachts, and giving employment to nearly 2,000
feamen.   No yacht under thirty tons is enrolled in the Club.

The annual regatta is one of the events of the feafon, drawing nearly all Englifh yachting men to the ifle in Auguft, and attracting year after year a greater number of foreigners. In fact, the fplendour of the Cowes yachts has afforded the younger Dumas an opening for a fcene in his comedy entitled "The Prodigal Father." It is a queftion of taking fome ladies of quality a fea-trip, from one of the fea-fide reforts upon the northern coaft of France—Dieppe.

"Tell me, young man," fays the extravagant father of the comedy, "how would you manage if you were permitted to conduct the marchionefs and her niece, who have a fancy for a trip on the fea, from this place to Tréport?"

"I fhould manage very fimply. I fhould call a fifherman, and hire his boat."

"And you think you would thereby act like a gentleman? You hand a couple of ladies into a fifhing fmack, fmelling of fifh and pitch, and you think you have done your duty!"

"What elfe could I do?"

"Liften; this is what I fhould do. I fhould fend a defpatch to White, the great Englifh yacht builder at Cowes, ordering him to bring over a yacht at once, manned, equipped, and quite ready—a veffel fit for ladies."

Eaft Cowes is not fo profperous as its fellow, otherwife its defcription is fimply a repetition of that of Weft Cowes—yachting, failors, a fearching fmell of fhips' provifions, and quantities of oil-fkin.

High up in the town the vifitor will find a Botanic Garden. There is also an Eaft Cowes Caftle, but not the one built by Henry VIII., correfponding to that of Weft Cowes. Not a veftige of this building remains. Grofe in his *Antiquities* fays:—"This has been long totally demolifhed; the materials have from time to time been carried away, fome within the

memory of perfons now living, in order to build a houfe at
Newport, and for other erections."

Both Weft and Eaft Cowes are well provided with places of
worfhip for all denominations. At Eaft Cowes the Trinity mafters
have a houfe, while Her Majefty poffeffes a private landing-place.

From Newport to Whippingham is a delightful walk, thus
defcribed by Charles Knight:—"The rambler may very well
keep befide the river to Whippingham, occafionally afcending
the uplands; and if he be a lover of river fcenery, he will not
regret the devious courfe it has led him. The broad fweep of
the ftream ftretches before you in bold fweeping curves, its clear
green water curling into light ripples, and reflecting in long
tremulous lines the white fails that are gliding rapidly along;
on each fide are fine hanging woods, or flopes of 'glad light
green.' In front the view is bounded by foftly-fwelling uplands,
or when a turn in the path brings into fight the broad opening
where the river falls into the fea, by the filver Solent, and the
hazy coaft beyond."

Whippingham Church is a charmed place, as being that now
ufed through many years by the Queen as her place of worfhip
when in the ifle. But the old building was fwept away to
make room for a new edifice, the firft ftone of which was laid
by Her Majefty seven months, almoft to a day, before the
Prince Confort expired. The act was one of the laft royal
public works previous to that great cataftrophe. The old
church was not of extraordinary architectural intereft, but it
was much vifited by reafon of its affociations with the royal
family of England. Knight fays of the old building:—"The
only poffible thing to notice infide would be its fcrupulous
cleanness. Now, of courfe, the royal pews are looked at by
the ftranger, but they are quiet and unaffuming, only diftinguifhed from the reft by a rather richer lining."

Ofborne.

SBORNE is derived from Aufterburne. The eftate which formed a nucleus for the 5,000 acres now comprifed in the word Ofborne, was the hereditary land of the Bowermans through many generations. From them it paffed through the hands of the Arneys to the Lovibonds, who held it until the time of Charles I., when it paffed into the poffeffion of Euftace Mann, about whofe memory is told one of thofe treafure tales with which Quarr is affociated. It is said that Mann buried a large fum of money in a wood near his houfe, and never could find the fpot beneath which the treafure lay. The tradition will not hold water, but the common people in fupport of their belief, triumphantly point to the fact that the fpot is called to this day Money Coppice. No doubt many a ruftic, when that part of the ifle was lefs ftrictly guarded than it now is, has fought in a defultory way for the loft treafure. If it has been found, no whifper of the difcovery has reached the general ear. The grand-daughter of this Euftace Mann married a Mr. Blachford, whofe fon built Ofborne House, a manfion of fome architectural pretenfion. It was a defcendant of this gentleman, the Lady Ifabella Blachford, who fold the eftate to the Queen in 1840. By fubfequent purchafes, it now extends almoft from the Medina on the weft, to King's Quay on the eaft; and here at King's Quay, it is faid, John King of England remained in hiding for fome time, when threatened

OSBORNE.

by the barons; hence the name, King's Quay. Indeed, feveral ifolated atoms of traditional evidence go to prove that John muft unqueftionably have vifited the ifland.

The old unpretending houfe was pulled down, and the handfome Italian building which now occupies its fite erected in its ftead. It is believed that the architecture of Ofborne is almoft wholly due to the late Prince Confort. The two towers, which

can be seen quite readily from Spithead, anfwer the purpofe—
the one (90 feet high) of a campanile or bell tower, the other
(107 feet in height) of a flag tower.

The Queen's apartments face the fea, but it is faid Her
Majefty's great delight when at Ofborne is to pafs much of
her time, when the weather will permit, upon one or other of
the flat terrace roofs with which the houfe abounds. In the
photograph the Queen's rooms are thofe on the right, fituated
before the flag tower.

Vifitors are fo rigoroufly excluded from the palace and
grounds of Ofborne, that very little is known concerning
either. The gardens are effentially of the terrace order, and
they flope almoft to the water's edge. The houfe itfelf is
crowded with works of art, and efpecially examples of fculpture
by the greateft fculptors in the Englifh fchool.

But if, on the one hand, the public are excluded from the
palace and park of Ofborne, on the other hand it muft be felt
that the intereft the Queen took in the eftablifhment of the
model farm, was, up to the time of the Prince Confort's death,
boundlefs and conftant. Upon that model farm was conducted
a feries of experiments which we have no doubt muft have
refulted in a great advance in agricultural knowledge had the
promoter been fpared to continue his work. As it happened
there was no time afforded to admit of refults, and there remains but the commencement of a great work. Every farmer
in the vicinity, who had an opportunity of exercifing his
judgment, will bear teftimony to the extraordinary vigour and
fkill with which the Prince's agricultural experiments were
carried on. Nor was fport forgotten : the eftate ftill maintains
fome excellent kennels.

The Ofborne lodges on the Eaft Cowes road are of fingularly fanciful defign. Ofborne muft not be left without fome

reference to the one chapter of antiquity in connection with the place. One of the estates abforbed into the royal demefne was that of Barton Manor. Coming, almost immediately after the Conquest, into the hands of the Fitz Sturs, their heirefs, in the reign of Henry III., married one Walter de Infula, who, very obvioufly by his name, had been born on the ifle. Shortly afterwards, in 1272, John de Infula, his brother, founded here a religious houfe, endowed it nobly, and dedicated it to the Trinity. The conftitution of this eftablifhment, preferved at Winchefter, gives an antiquarian intereft to the fpot. Here is a copy of it.

" 1. There fhall be fix chaplains and one clerk, to officiate both for the living and the dead, under the rules of St. Augus-. tine. 2. One of thefe fhall be prefented to the Bifhop of Winchefter to be the arch-prieft, to whom the reft fhall take an oath of obedience. 3. The arch-prieft fhall be chofen by the chaplains there refiding, who fhall prefent him to the bifhop within twenty days after any vacancy fhall happen. 4. They fhall be fubject to the immediate authority of the bifhop. 5. When any chaplain fhall die, his goods fhall remain in the oratory. 6. They fhall have only one mefs, with a pittance at a meal, excepting on the greater feftivals, when they may have three meffes. 7. They fhall be diligent in reading and pray-ing. 8. They fhall not go beyond the bounds of the oratory without licence from the arch-prieft. 9. Their habits fhall be of one colour, either blue or black ; they fhall be clothed *pallio Hibernienfi de nigra boneta cum pileo* (in the Irifh veftment of a black bonnet and a cloak). 10. The arch-prieft fhall fit at the head of the table, next to him thofe who have celebrated the great mafs, then the prieft of St. Mary, next the prieft of the Holy Trinity, and then the prieft who fays mafs for the dead. 11. The clerk fhall read fomething edifying to them

P

while they dine.   12. They fhall fleep in one room.   13. They
fhall make fpecial prayer for their benefactors.   14. They fhall,
in all their ceremonies, and in tinkling the bell, follow the ufe
of Sarum.   15. The arch-prieft alone fhall have charge of the
bufinefs of the houfe.   16. All of them, after their admiffion
into the houfe, fhall fwear to obferve these ftatutes.   *Further
Ordered:*—After a year and a day from entering into the oratory,
no one fhall accept of any other benefice, or fhall depart the
houfe."

Upon the diffolution of religious eftablifhments, this of the
Holy Trinity fell to pieces, and ultimately upon its fite, or near
it, was built in the time of Elizabeth, Barton Court, which
remained in partial exiftence until pulled down on its purchafe
by Her Majefty.

Moody fays of this building :—" One peculiarity of the houfe
was, that it contained a room about twelve feet fquare, known
as the Chapel, which had been apparently fitted up as a fecret
chapel for the performance of mafs, fubfequent to the Reformation, and which, within the memory of living individuals,
retained its altar, crucifix, and other Catholic acceffories."
Some portions of the old building, its fouthern and its eaftern
front, were however, retained, and now form part of the royal
refidence.

Newport.

———◆◇◆———

EAVING Ofborne, Whippingham Church neftles in a hollow in front, while the land is dotted with the red brick buildings occupied by the royal labourers' cottages. They are pleafant little buildings, yet with that model look about them which is fo comfortlefs. Throughout, there are evidences of the intereft taken by Her Majefty and the Prince in the improvement of the eftate. The labourers meet you with perfeĉt fimplici:y, yet with a full knowledge that they are a fort of fhow folk. Here we find the praĉtical out-crop of royalty in our time. It leans to agriculture, to making itfelf one with others, to its being people amongft the people, and to poffefling interefts identical with theirs.

It is well to turn from the fmiling acres, the undulating valleys, and the red brick cots, to the left, and look upon that frowning caftle which now comes in view. A great contraft —on the one hand the heavy walls, on the other the royalty of to-day. Where are thofe old caftles, with their thick-hided miftruft? The moats are dry, the bridges have fallen, the portcullifes are rufted, and the walls are crumbling:—colonies for half-ftarved owls, jays, rooks, and magpies; the whole placed in the feeble care of fome poor aged retainer, who totters over the place, and opens the outer door with a rufty key. The defcendants of the caftellans have gone into civilifed houfes, and as to their fuccefs, the anfwer is in the fmiling acres around Ofborne, and in the quiet manner in which the Queen drives about the ifland.

Suddenly the traveller faces Newport—Whippingham fteeple is loft—Whippingham, which owns a chapelry that pays ten fhillings a year in acknowledgment of its dependency. And now we face the hill crowned by Carifbrook Caftle.

The firft warning Carifbrook had of its fate, was when Ifabel fold the ifle to the Englifh crown. Hitherto Newport was the village. Carifbrook, neftling under the Caftle, was the capital of the ifland. But with the fale Carifbrook loft its importance as the refidence of a feudal baron, and with that importance fell what power was poffeffed by the Priory, a power which well competed with that of Quarr.

Newport now began to rife in importance, for while the mif-truftful Caftle was on a hill, Newport was fituated more wifely on a river, and its boats foon began to be bufy carrying the corn and hay grown in the heart of the ifle, and bringing back such commodities as foreign lands and diftant London had to offer. Soon the fong of the water-mill was heard upon the banks of the river, and Carifbrook began to fall to pieces. However, the brave old place ftill holds up its hoary head. A couple of modern cannon would fend it into a heap of rubbifh in an hour, but there being no need to interfere with its green old age, it remains a pleafant end to a tourift's jaunt.

Newport is, loofely fpeaking, nearly in the centre of the ifland,

and advantageously situated for commerce, which here has never, from the time of the Reformation, ceased steadily to increase.

The Medina, the river upon which Newport lies, is navigable up to the town for small craft only, but the power of the engineer has been felt in some degree, as in almost all parts of England.

Newport exports corn, which is carried down to Cowes, where it is re-shipped, the return cargoes consisting of coal, iron, timber, and groceries; for Newport is the centre whence the interior and back of the island are supplied with their daily luxuries.

In the time of good Sir Richard Worsley, that baronet was proud to make the record, that on market-day, every Saturday, not fewer than 200 waggon loads of various kinds of grain were brought into the town, amounting to from 1,300 to 1,500 quarters, the greater part of which remained on the island until converted into ships' bread, or rather biscuit, which was preferably bought up for the English navy.

Newport itself is not very striking, for there is no building within its boundaries calling for high admiration, while the houses themselves have little of the quaintness of age to recommend them. The town, however, is wide and open, while its several squares give it an airy appearance which is much in its favour.

The ancient Church of St. Thomas à Becket must have been established about 1180, the founder being Richard de Redvers, a pious soul, who covenanted with the priory at Carisbrook, that two monks should pray at St. Thomas's daily. The building was due to much brotherly effort, for every guild in the town gave the church a helping hand, and hence it came to pass, that the distinguishing signs of each company were carved upon the exterior walls. It remained a chapelry of Carifbrook until very recently. Newport alfo poffeffes the power of appointing its own minifter, who at one time depended upon voluntary contributions, but at a later date upon a town rate. However, the burgeffes ftrove, even fo early as the time of the unhappy Charles I, to render Newport parochial, but without fuccefs. Many were the petitions forwarded to Parliament in the endeavour to obtain this advantage—petitions that were confidered, and practically put on one fide.

Here is a copy of one of the petitions in queftion.

"*The humble Petition of the Maior and Burgeffes, and other cheife inhabitants of the Burrough of Newport, in the Ifle of Wight, Sheweth:—*

"1. That the faid Burough is a Corporation, a port Towne, and auntient Markett Towne, wᶜʰ ferveth the whole Ifle of Wight. Seated in the hart of the Ifland, confifting of about three thoufand foules there in habitant, adourned wᵗʰ a very convenient Church lately enlarged, and well-fitted, and bewtified by the greate expenfe of the Inhabitants.

"2. That the faid Church being called St. Thomas Chappell is but a Chappell of Ease unto the p'ifh of Carifbrooke, wᶜʰ is a greater p'ifh, the viccarage thereof, wᵗʰ the other profitts thereto belonging, being reputed to be worth twoe hundred pounds at the leaft, and the obventions, oblations, and proffitts due to the Vicar, out of Newport, xxˡⁱ pound, or thereabouts, whereof Mr. Alexander Roffe, the nowe Incumbent (liveing out of the Ifland), alloweth but ten pounds pr annum to the newe curate, namely Mr. William Harby, Mafter of Arts, an able and laborious preacher, and a man of honeft converfation, whoe for the time of his abode in Newport, being about twelve yeares, hath not omitted preaching there on any Saboth day (unlefs by ficknefs or other neceffity he hath been p'vented).

"3. That the cure of foules in Newport hath been but meanly ferved in times paft, and like enough would be foe nowe, did not the Inhabitants, by a voluntary benevolence to the faid Mr. Harby make an addition to his meanes to keepe him wᵗʰ them. And it is greatly feared that in time to come the Inhabitants may fuffer much want of fpirituall foode for their foules—if their preachers means be not augmented.

"Y^r Pet^{rs} therefore moft humbly pray that the p'miffes may be taken
into y^r hob'e and pious confideration. And that y^t may be enacted and
fettled by Parliam^t, if that high and hob^{le} houfe think it convenient, that the
faid Buirough of Newport may be a diftinct p'ifh of ytfelf. And that y^{or}
Pet^{rs} and their fucceffors may have the p'entation of the parfon thereof for
ever, wch if it may be obteyned, y^r Pet^{rs} (albeit the town is very poor, and
they have been at extraordinarie charge already unto the church) yet for the
advancem^t of preaching the Word of God in the fame Burrough they are
very willing that it be alfo enacted that tweive pence of every pound of the
yearly rents of the houfes and lands within the faid Burrough (wch it is
confidered will amount to a competency) fhall be rayfed for an addition of
means to the parson of the faid Burrough for perpetuity, wch y^{or} Pet^{rs} con-
ceive will be a great work of piety, and muft tend to the glory of Almighty
God, the greate comforte of the fouls of his people in the said Burrough
inhabiting and thither reforting ffor wch y Pet^{rs} fhall ever be bound to
thankfulnefs."

This petition is dated February 1, 1640.

Nine years before its date a rich inhabitant, being a burgefs
of Newport, had beftowed upon the church a new and fantaftic
pulpit, carved by one Caper, an appropriate name, who ufed
an appropriate fymbol of himfelf upon the carved wood, in
the fhape of a carved goat. This pulpit is ftill to be feen in
the new church, which was built upon the fite of the ancient
building.

One William Pavey, who flourifhed in 1718-19, gives a
very elaborate defcription of this old church, dedicated to
Thomas à Becket.

"The church is like, at firft view, three ridged houfes joined, embattled
on the top. On the upper part are five windows between fix leaden fpouts,
and underneath four large windows, with a large porch, which is the grand
entrance, in the middle of the fouth fide. The tower is pretty lofty, and
embattled with four pinnacles.

"Within the church is one of the moft curious carved *pulpits* that I ever
faw, the work of one Thomas Caper (who now lies buried in Salifbury),
Ano. Dm. 1630, in which year the feats likewife were erected. It was a

donation of one Stephen March, whofe creft is againft the back of the pulpit.*
As for the carving, round the founding board of it is this infcription in neat,
wrought, and gilded letters: '*Cry aloud and fpare not*; *lift up thy voice like
a trumpet.*' The pulpit is divided into two rows of baf-relief carved images.
On the uppermoft row are curioufly defcribed the four Cardinal Virtues and
the three Graces, with their types; and on the lower rank the feven liberal
fciences—namely Grammatica, Dialectica, Rhetorica, Mufica, Arithmetica
Geometria, and Aftronomia, with the feveral fymbols and characteriftics of
each fcience. 'Tis a true church militant, for there is a canon placed to
defend the church now it is in danger. Nothing more remarkable in it, but
a neat, light grey marble front. [This is in the new building, and bears
an infcription—'*The givet of Anne Keith, Widow*, 1637.']

"Underneath the ftep that goes up to the altar is the vault wherein is interred the *Lady Elizabeth*, daughter to King Charles I.; and this is the
infcription, as Mr. John Gilbert, jun., told me:—

"'THE LADY ELIZABETH, DAUGHTER TO KING CHARLES THE 1ST,
SEPT. 8, MDCL.'

"Againft the fouth wall is the famed tomb of Sir Edward Horfley, Knt.,
who was often fent thither in Henry VIII.'s time, to defend it from any
fudden invafion from France. It is a curious marble monument, on which
lies his effigies at length, armed at all points complete, with his hands held
up, and joined in a praying manner, and on an oval piece of black marble
this epitaph:—

> " ' Edvardvs qvi miles erat fortiffimvs Horfey.
>   Veftis eiat præfes, conftans terraq. mariq.
>   Magnanimvs placidæ fvb pacis nomine fortis
>   Jvftitiæ Cvltor qvam fidvs amicvs amico
>   Favtor Evangelii delectvs Principe vixit
>   Mvnificvs Popvlo mvltvm delectvs ab omni
>   Vixit et vt fancte fic ftamina fancte peregit.'

> " ' Qvi ob. 23 die Marcii,
>   Anno Domini 1582."

"This is all that is worth notice in the Church.

"In the church-yard, which is about a quarter of a mile weft of the
church, neatly walled in, are the following remarkable infcriptions:—

"'Here lyeth the body of Mastr George Shergold, late Minifter of New-

---

* Was the goat the creft of Stephen March, or a punning fymbol of the carver's
name? Perhaps it meant both.

port, who, during fixteen years in difcharge of his office, ftrictly obferved the true difcipline of the Church of England difliking that dead bodies fhould be buried in God's houfe, appointed to be interred in this place. He dyed univerfally lamented and efteemed, January 23, 1707.'

" On a head-ftone on the fouth fide of the church-yard, this:—

"'Here lyeth ye body of John Smith, who departed this life ye 12th day of Auguft, in ye year of our Lord 1712, in ye 24th year of his age.'

> " ' Stay, gentle reader, fpend a tear
> Upon ye duft y^t fleepeth ere ;
> And whilft thou read'ft ye ftate of me,
> Think on ye glafs y^t runs for thee.' "

" On a brafs plate on a fine raifed tomb near ye middle of ye church-yard:—

"'Here is laid ye body of Mr. John Stanner, who departed this life ye 26th of March, 1713, in ye 65th year of his age: a man exemplary for piety, and forward in works of charity, efpecially worthy of a good and lafting (*fic*) for an act of gratitude more than common, as in return for a feafonable (tho' noe great) benefaction, he bequeathed ye greateft fhare of his eftate (gotten by an honeft induftry) to come to ye great-grandchildren of that his benefactor.'

" See by this how ye bread that a man may have caft upon ye waves cometh to be again found after many days."

It was in 1853-4, not very many years after Her Majefty had acquired the Ofborne eftate, that the old church of St. Thomas exhibited fuch unequivocal figns of decay that its demolition became an abfolute neceffity. Already the royal family had identified themfelves moft heartily with all fchemes tending to the advancement of the ifland, and therefore the Prince Confort readily confented to officiate at the laying of the foundation ftone of the new building, which was placed on Auguft 24th, 1854. The works were fo vigoroufly carried on that the edifice was opened for divine worfhip in 1856. By that time £10,000 had been laid out upon the building. The church is in the ftyle known as Early Englifh. It exhibits much harmony; it is light, elegant, and worthy of its architect, Mr. Daukes.

Q

The monuments which gave fo great an intereft to the ancient church were replaced in the new building. And now it was that Her Majefty fhowed the tender memory in which fhe held that royal unfortunate, the Princefs Elizabeth. Here, in the new church of St. Thomas, fhe has erected a monument in memory of that unhappy princefs, who, at a very early age, muft have welcomed death as a fweet relief. The monument is one of the moft fuccefsful works of the late Baron Marochetti. It reprefents the princefs lying dead under the window of her prifon, which they fhow you at Carifbrook, her head pillowed upon a Bible as fhe was found by the jailors who watched her. The likenefs is from a portrait in the poffeffion of Her Majefty, and the following infcription completes the work :—" To the memory of the Princefs Elizabeth, daughter of Charles I., who died at Carifbrook Caftle on Sunday, Sept. 8th, 1650, and is interred beneath the chancel of this church, this monument is erected—a token of refpect for her virtues, and of fympathy for her misfortunes—by Victoria R., 1856."

Speaking of this princefs, Clarendon fays:—"She was a lady of diftinguifhed parts, of quick obfervation, and early under-ftanding." She fank into an early grave at the age of fifteen, three of which fhe had paffed in confinement. Hume fays it was intended by her Puritan jailors to have apprenticed the princefs to a button-maker in Newport, but the ftatement utterly lacks evidence. "*Vatene in pace alma beata e bella.*" She expired about nineteen months after the execution of the king, dying no doubt all the time. It was fo late as 1793 that the remains were difcovered in a vault near the altar. A ftone bearing the letters E. S. (Elizabeth Stuart) marked the fpot. The vault was perfectly dry, and contained a leaden coffin, which appeared as though new, and bore this infcription—

a ftrangely royal one for her parliamentary undertakers to place
upon it—

ELIZABETH 2D DAVGHTER

OF Yᴱ LATE KING CHARLES

Dece'd Sept. 8 MDCL.

A kindlier epitaph followed, two centuries being paft.

Up to the time of Elizabeth the dead of Newport were
carried to Carifbrook, but during the life of that monarch, an
epidemic raging in Newport, the burial ground at Carifbrook
was found too narrow, and the people of Newport, turning
their attention to the formation of a graveyard of their own,
obtained the grant of a ftretch of land on the fouth fide of the
town, which is ufed as a cemetery to this day.

Newport is a market town and a borough ; Saturday is the
general market day, and to the market the whole produce of
the ifland is brought. Upon every other Wednefday a cattle
market is held. The annual fair, which is dying out, as all
annual fairs are expiring, is held every Whit-Monday and two
following days. Newport has a jurifdiction of its own, holds
a court of borough petty feffions every Monday, and county
petty feffions every Saturday. Once a month, alfo, a county
court for the ifland fits at Newport.

It was at the inftance of Sir George Carey, Governor of
the Ifle of Wight, that Newport was fummoned to return two
reprefentatives to Parliament in the 27th of Elizabeth, 1585.
From that date, when candidates for parliamentary honours were
far from plentiful, to the prefent time, Newport has always
been regularly reprefented. However, it muft be admitted
that until the operation of the firft Reform Act Newport
was unqueftionably a clofe borough, for the right of voting had
till then been confined to free burgeffes, the number of thefe
being reftricted to twenty-four. Hence it followed that lefs

than two dozen votes could return a couple of members to the Houſe of Commons. The conſtituency has had the honour of returning to parliament, amongſt its more diſtinguiſhed repreſentatives, the late Lord Palmerſton (1790-1807), and the Right Hon. George Canning (1826). By the Reform Act (1868) one member has been taken away.

The population is a little over eight thouſand. Nor is the corporation of Newport in an unflouriſhing condition. A few years ſince its income amounted to £1,054, while its expenditure was only £543.

Newport, amongſt other advantages of civilization, poſſeſſes a fire brigade, worked at the ſmall annual expenditure of £60, and this although the brigade conſiſts of a ſuperintendent, three engineers, three foremen, and five firemen.

Amongſt the public buildings of Newport, the *Town Hall*, a heavy but ſubſtantial building, is noticeable. The *Free Grammar School* is a plain building, intereſting from the facts that here Charles I. met the Parliamentary Commiſſioners in 1648, and that in the chamber now uſed as a ſchool-room divine ſervice was, in the early part of the royal impriſonment, performed before the hapleſs king and his ſuite. The ſchool, which owes its exiſtence chiefly to good Sir Thomas Oglander (and the Oglander MSS. relating to the iſle have ſtill to be publiſhed—no doubt they will one day ſee the light), was intended for the education on the foundation of fifteen (now twenty) boys, who ſtill enter at from ſeven to eight years of age, and quit at fifteen. The ſchool alſo receives thirty day ſcholars, while the maſter may receive boarders. The chief reliable income of the eſtabliſhment ariſes from the rent of three houſes in Newport, and of about 35 acres of land at Hemmy Hill. The nominal ſalary given to the maſter is £120, together with a rent-free houſe and garden.

The Ifle of Wight Mufeum is to be found in what may be candidly ftyled a barn, and where it is ftrangely mixed up with newfpapers and a bagatelle board. That from an archæological point of view the mufeum is moft interefting, there can be no doubt, but the apparent curatrefs—a maiden whofe chief duty appears to be the quieting of her young charge by giving the infant the more attractive objects in the mufeum for playthings—exhibits, as the chief curiofities of the place, a wafps' neft, and fome frightfully ftuffed animals congenitally malformed.

The true curator, however, drew up a very interefting paper having reference to the antiquarian treafures poffeffed by the mufeum. We make the following extracts from that compilation :—

"The hiftorical and antiquarian department contains : Cafe 1. A large funereal urn, taken from a Britifh or Celtic *barrow* on Shalcombe Down, meafuring 16 inches by 14; feveral incineratories from fimilar barrows opened in various parts of the ifland; ancient Celtic torques; *celts* found at Binftead, Watchingwell, Billingham, &c.; a large collection of pottery from a Romano-Britifh manufactory at Barnes, near Brixton, confifting of fragments of urns, pateras, and other utenfils, fome fpecimens being nearly entire. The moft interefting feature is its variety, the collection appertaining to feveral hiftorical eras. The earlieft fpecimens are of a coarfe, flightly baked pottery, fimilar to that of the Britifh or Celtic period. A fecond variety is Samian ware. The third differs in no refpect from the urns found in various Saxon barrows in the ifland. Many are plain.

"Cafe II. contains fragments of Celtic funeral urns, with incinerations, found near Yafford and on Compton Down; an ancient Britifh or Celtic bronze inftrument, or dagger, and pottery found in a barrow opened on Arreton Down; a collection of Anglo-Saxon remains difcovered in various ifland barrows and in the cemetery on Cheffell Down, and prefented by the late Sir Leonard Worfley Holmes, Mr. Bennett, and other gentlemen. The moft interefting are iron fwords and knives; iron fpear-heads for warfare, and the fports of the chafe.

"Another Cafe contains Ifle of Wight trade-tokens; Englifh local tokens and half-pence; large and fmall brafs coins, Roman and Greek, not difcovered in the ifland.

" Case IV. contains 170 filver, and large and fmall brafs Roman and Greek Coins (from Auguftus Cæfar, A.D. 31, to Gratian, A.D. 313), found in various parts of the ifland.

" In a recefs are various interefting relics of the ancient chapel of St. Thomas, Newport, and a collection of human bones of former Anglo-Saxon inhabitants.

" In a room adjacent is a model of old St. Thomas' Church ; fpecimens of Roman fculpture found among its materials ; Roman tiles, bricks, and mortar from Carifbrook ; steel dies of a fixpence and a fhilling, formerly coined at Newport ; a collection of ancient weapons ; ancient fword, &c., &c."

The Ifle of Wight Inftitution is an elegant structure, and contains an excellent library of 5,000 volumes.

It is typical of the old feudal dependency of Newport upon Carifbrook, that the mayor of the town is fworn in (on Michaelmas Day) at Carifbrook Caftle, before the fteward and governor of the ifle. The corporation confifts of the mayor, fix aldermen, and eighteen councillors, from amongft whom the aldermen are chofen.

Newport received its firft charter from Richard de Redvers, a defcendant of the firft lord of Wight, and who himfelf was lord of the ifle in the time of Henry II. Ifabella de Fortibus, fhe who afterwards fold the ifle to the Englifh crown, gave a fword and very liberal charter to " her" new borough of Newport, while between Richard II. and Charles II. no lefs than fifteen charters were granted to the borough, all of which are extant, the parchments in many cafes containing portraits of the fovereigns in whofe reigns they were granted. In Charles II.'s time a recorder was appointed to Newport.

Some antiquarians maintain, probably with juftice, that Newport, when called Medi, was a Roman fettlement of much importance. " Both here," fays the Rev. E. Kell, " and in other parts of the ifland, have been found vafes, gems, rings,

fibulæ, fwords, coins, bracelets, and urns. The coins dis-
covered in different quarters range over the whole period of
the Roman occupation of Britain, and even defcend to a later
date. The Romans left England in A.D. 414 to 420; and yet
at Shanklin, in 1833, were difcovered coins of the emperors
Arcadius and Honorius; and the latter did not reign until
A.D. 424."

In 1377 Newport fell efpecially upon evil times, for it
yielded to the French, who however, as we have elfewhere
fhown, were repulfed with great flaughter, upon their attempt
to take Carifbrook by affault. Again, in the time of Edward
IV., the town fuffered from another fuccefsful attack on the
part of the French.

But it was in Elizabeth's reign that the moft evil days
Newport ever knew almoft overwhelmed the borough. The
plague decimated the inhabitants, the dead carts blocked the
way to Carifbrook, the graveyard there could hold no more
dead, and defolation and defpair haunted every corner of the
town.

However, with the elafticity of the Englifh charaéter, Newport and its men rofe fuperior to their misfortunes, and to
greater profperity than before. Soon after that time of trouble,
we have Sir John Oglander tellirg, in his MSS., how he had
known as many as " twelve knights and as many other gentlemen" to attend in the firft town hall that the men of Newport
built.

In a report of the condition of the ifland drawn up in 1642,
we find the following paffage :—

"Since yᵉ coming of King James, there is a toun in the ifland (called
Newport) made a mare-toun, which heretofore was only a bayly-toun, and
then yᵉ live-tenants and juftices had yᵉ fame power there they had in
yᵉ reft of yᵉ country. But now they have gotten a charter to be a mare-

toun, and have juſtices, a recorder, aldermen, &c., which yᵉ other two mare-
touns have not, as Yarmouth and Newtoun ; they will not be governed as
thoſe two mare-touns and yᵉ reſt of ye iſland are, which is very prejudiciall
to yᵉ country, and I wiſh it might be regulated. And in that toun of Newport yᵉ captain of ye iſland is clerk of yᵉ market, and hath yᵉ ordering of
yᵉ country; this toun, notwithſtanding, will take yᵉ puwer to themſelves,
and hinder men from buying and ſelling at their pleaſure."

Newport remained very excluſive long after a more liberal
municipal policy had been recognized over the greater part of the
kingdom. So late as 1629 we find the corporation oppoſing
one John Wavell, in his deſire to open a certain ſhop, the
argument held by the corporation being that he had not ſerved
his apprenticeſhip in the town. Ultimately John Wavell was
permitted to trade, upon conſenting to pay an exemplary fine.

The Charities of Newport conſiſt of the Blue School,
formed in 1781, for the education and maintenance of twenty
poor girls born in Newport, to be made " good Chriſtians and
uſeful ſubjeċts." 'Tis a quaint old ſchool, ſupported by voluntary contributions and the intereſts of certain bequeſts. The
ſchool is managed by the miniſter of Newport, aided by ſix
ladies. Every girl, upon leaving the eſtabliſhment, is preſented
with clothes, a Prayer Book, and Bible ; while farthermore,
let her but keep her firſt ſituation twelve months, and ſhe is
entitled to a guinea.

Worſley's almſhouſes were founded in 1618, by Sir R.
Worſley, and through proviſion of the will of Giles Kent.
It is true they conſiſt of but ſix ſmall rooms, a tenant in each,
but they are always full.

Widow Roman's almſhouſes, built in 1752, owe their exiſtence to the following clauſe in the good woman's will:—" I
bequeath to ſuch ſix widows as ſhall inhabit the Charity Houſe
in Newport, called the Lower Almſhouſe, ſituated in Crocker
Street, and ſhall not receive alms from the town, the ſum of

£10 every year for ever after the deceafe of my brother-in-law, W. Roman, from my property at Yafford, free from all taxes and deductions whatever; by equal portions, by the church-wardens and overfeers of the poor of the parifh of Newport, to be difpofed of to the fix widows equally, fhare and fhare alike."

The Upper Almfhoufes are four tenements, a family in each, founded in 1623, by one Daniel Serle, a parifhioner of Caris-brook.

Finally, it is argued in favour of Newport that the general plan of the town is effentially that of a Roman city, and that therefore its prefent linear afpect is very much what it was in the fecond and third centuries. Nor is the borough without its modern admirers.

Mudie fays :—" Newport is effentially a domeftic town—the heart and centre of the Ifle of Wight. Its ftreets are laid out with great regularity, lying eaft and weft, with crofs ones north and fouth, dividing the area into chequers. The two principal are thofe which connect the great roads—St James's Street, from Cowes road, to that which leads by Nizon to the Under-cliff; and High Street, which connects the Ryde road with the road to Carifbrook, and the weftern roads which diverge from them."

Knight alfo gives his teftimony in favour of the town :—" Newport ftands nearly in the centre of the ifland, in a fpot apparently marked out by nature for the fite of the miniature capital. It is built on a gentle flope rifing from the weft bank of the Medina, which is navigable for veffels of confiderable burden up to the town; and the nature of the furrounding hills allows of eafy lines of communication to radiate from it to every part of the ifland. The town itfelf is neat, clean, cheerful-looking, and apparently flourifhing. The ftreets are well paved and lighted, and filled with good, well-ftored fhops."

R

Shanklin.

———•◦•———

"HE diſtance," says Mantell, "from Bembridge Down to Shanklin is from four to five miles. On the eaſtern ſide of Sandown Bay, the flinty chalk has a total thicknefs of 200 feet, the lower chalk and chalk marl 200 feet, the fireſtone 100 feet, and the galt 50 feet."

The eye ſoon reſts upon Redcliff, and here the ſtrata firſt viſible are the ferruginous ſandy and mottled clays, belonging to the Wealden formation, which becomes more developed as we look towards the chalk ſtrata terminating in the bold promontory of Culver, which forms a ſtriking objeƈt from this part of the bay. In the Wealden, bones of large reptiles and fruits of coniferous plants have from time to time been diſcovered, and many coloſſal bones of the iguanodon have been obtained from the ſhingle, where alſo may be found rolled blocks and pebbles of the ſhelly limeſtones, and of jaſper and quartz, with ſilicified zoophytes, that have been waſhed out of the chalk. Slabs of what is commonly called

FRANKLIN PINE

Suffex marble may alfo be' seen protruding from the clay; while maffes of lignite that have fallen out of the cliffs are often found on the beach, and fometimes pebbles of filicified wood.

The occurrence in this locality of bones of the iguanodon and other reptiles, whofe remains had previoufly been obferved only in the ftrata of Tilgate Foreft, was firft made known in 1829, by Dr. Buckland. An enormous toe-bone, weighing fix pounds, and meafuring fix inches in length, and fixteen inches in circumference at its largeft extremity, was found in the ledges of ferruginous fand, a little to the eaft of Sandown Fort, while a confiderable number of bones, com-prifing feveral gigantic vertebræ, portions of a thigh bone, frag-ments of ribs, &c., were difcovered near the fame fpot—at the foot of the low cliff that forms the fea boundary of Yaverland farm. They were obferved on the fhore after a week of very ftormy weather, which had fwept away the beach and fand to the depth of two feet, and thus laid bare the foffils which pro-bably had fallen from the cliffs long previoufly, and being very heavy had funk deep into the fhingle, and lain concealed until brought to light by the denuding effects of a ftorm.

A fharp walk, and we are at Shanklin.

All who have feen leafy Shanklin fpeak tenderly of it. Who can avoid, who need avoid fpeaking gently of the fweet hanging curtains of green that clothe this lovely fpot. It is fo human, if we may be allowed the word. Blackgang is ghaftly in its barrenness and its remorfelefs divorce from vegetation. Shanklin is fweet with fhadow, leafy twitterings, the murmur of a prat-tling ftreamlet, and the fall of a tiny waterfall. Nay, the very prefence of the little perched-up heavy-browed inn, the woman with her bafkets of pebble jewelry, which without a blufh fhe tells you is all made on the ifle from ftones found on the beach, the gates, the feats, the ruftic bridge—all help to produce a fenfe of comfort, and give humanity to the fcene.

Water and time made a fearful gafh in the fide of a hill, men came and planted trees, made the place beautiful, and converted a wildernefs into a garden. This is Shanklin.

"Shanklin," fays Keats, " is a moft beautiful place. Sloping wood and meadow ground reach round the chine, which is a cleft in the cliffs of the depth of nearly 300 feet. This cleft is filled with trees and bufhes in the narrow part, and as it widens becomes bare, if it were not for the primrofes on one fide, which fpread to the very verge of the fea, and fome fifhermen's huts on the other, perched midway in the baluftrade of beautiful green hedges along the fteps down to the fand."

The fifhermen's huts have long fince gone, and upon the fite of one of them are to be found feats, from which a perfect view, fomething in formation like the Bay of Naples, is to be feen fweeping round and up to Culver Cliffs.

Sir. H. Englefield has fpoken in terms of high praife of this natural beauty, the cliffs of which are 230 feet high, the chafm at the top 300 feet wide, while it ftretches back inland from the fhore 150 feet. But when Sir Henry wrote Shanklin had not been turned to the beft account. He fays :—" The cliff, where the ftream which forms the chine enters the fea, is about 100 feet in height, and the chafm is perhaps 150 wide at the top, and at the bottom not much wider than the channel of the ftream. The fides are very fteep, and in moft places are clothed with rich underwood, overhanging the naked rock. At a fmall diftance within their mouth, on a terrace juft large enough to afford a walk to their doors, ftand two fmall cottages of different elevations. Rude flights of fteps defcend to them from the top, and an excavation from the fandy rock forms a fkittle-ground to one of them, overfhadowed by the leafage of young oaks. After proceeding about 100 yards in a direct line from the shore, the chasm makes a sudden bend to the left, and grows much narrower. Its sides are nearly perpendicular, and but little shrubbery breaks their naked surface. The chasm continues decreasing in breadth, till it terminates in an extremely narrow fissure, down which the rill, which has formed the whole, falls about 30 feet. The quantity of water is in general so small that the cascade is

SHANKLIN CHURCH.

scarcely worth viewing; but after great rains it must be very pretty. The sides of the gloomy hollow in which it falls are of the blackish indurated clay, of which the greater part of the soil hereabouts is composed, and the damp of the water has covered most part of it with shining green lichens and mosses of various fhades. The brufhwood which grows on the brow on each fide, overhangs fo as nearly to meet; and the whole fcene, though it cannot be confidered as magnificent, is certainly ftriking and grotefque. Above the fall the ftream continues to run in a deep and fhady channel quite to the foot of the hills in which it takes its rife."

Lord Jeffrey, an accomplifhed critic, has alfo fpoken well of Shanklin. He remarks:—"Shanklin is very fmall and fcattery, all mixed up with trees, and lying among fweet airy falls and fwells of ground, which finally rife up behind to breezy downs 800 feet high, and fink down in front to the edge of the varying cliffs, which overhang a pretty beach of fine fand, and are approachable by a very ftriking wooded ravine, which they call the *Chine*."

Shanklin Chine, like all others in the ifland, has been formed by the action of running water. In fact, to be profaic, they are huge gulleys, dependent for their formation upon foft earth and rain ftreams. At Shanklin the farther cutting away of the earth is ftopped by the fimple ufe of a ftone flab on the edge of the cliff over which the rain has paffed for fo many centuries. The waterfall looks very pretty from below; and chatting with the half-agricultural, half-marine, friendly-faced fellow who keeps the gate, we take another mug of the flightly mineralized water, which here flows into a fmall ftone receptacle. The water is ferruginous. The keeper declares it faves children who are fuffering from rickets.

Along the fouth coaft of the ifland and the line of the chines, great attention was given by the military engineers who controlled the making of the military road from Frefhwater to Blackgang, now about ten years fince, to arreft the rapid action of even a very narrow ftream of water, in cutting a chine under favourable circumftances. The road is in fome parts carried over chines certainly at a height of two hundred feet. It was therefore neceſſary to ſtop the action of the water upon the land, or the waſting away of the foundations of the viaducts was but a queſtion of time—a queſtion which nature holds in little reſpect. The chine-cutting brooks, over which the road paſſed, were conſequently confined to artificial channels, and the danger is at all events poſtponed.

How eaſily a chine may be formed is to be gathered from an inſpection of Shepherd's Chine, an offshoot of Cowleaſe Chine. Fifty years ſince, a farm labourer, who gives his name to the chine—and this act is very typical of the ſimple and natural way in which a ſpot obtains a title—fifty years ſince this ſhepherd, for the amuſement of an idle minute, and having a ſpade in his hand, cut a gully on one ſide of the rivulet pouring down Cowleaſe Chine. The water took the new courſe at once, abandoned Cowleaſe, and commenced the formation of a new chine, which is already of reſpectable dimenſions.

To come back to Shanklin, the touriſt muſt not leave the ſpot without a look at the ſuperb girdle of myrtles which ſurrounds the venerable parſonage.

Luccombe Chine.

—•◦•—

HE walk at low water from Shanklin to Luccombe Chine is very pleafant. Luccombe
Chine is one of thofe places we find in every
route taken by tourifts, which are unaccount-
ably neglected although equally beautiful with
other much-praifed fpots. Here is Luccombe
Chine only fecond to that of Shanklin, and
not one tourift in a hundred of thofe who
vifit Shanklin sets an eye upon Luccombe.
Indeed, it is moft picturefque, and for thofe
who love the natural without any intrufion
of the artificial, Luccombe Chine is the moft
delightful in the ifle. Viewed from the fhore, it is fingularly
fweeping and beautiful, piled up fuperbly. But its entrance from
above is quite unaffuming. It fuddenly finks out of a field in
the moft unpretentious manner, opening out far below the
upper level. No fignpoft tells of its exiftence, and the prefence
of humanity is feebly reprefented by a few cottages. Luccombe Chine will well repay a paffing vifit, and fhould not be
overlooked by the tourift.

The Undercliff.

———•———

ND now we approach the great natural beauty of the Ifle of Wight—the Undercliff.

Sir James Clark, after a careful examination of various places on the Englifh coaft, decided that many invalids might find thofe benefits from climate clofe at home, which they feek in diftant countries. He, in faét, "MADE" the Undercliff.

He fays of it, in his work "The Influence of Climate on the Prevention and Cure of Chronic Difeafes":— "A lofty natural terrace, backed by a mountainous wall on the north, and open on the fouth to the full influence of the fun from his rifing to his going down, during that feafon when his influence is moft wanted in a northern country." And elfewhere he adds:—"The ifland, from the variety which it prefents in point of elevation, foil, and afpeét, and from the configuration of its hills and fhores, poffeffes feveral peculiarities of climate and fituation, which render it a very favourable and commodious refidence throughout the year, for a large clafs of invalids. On this account, the Ifle of Wight claims

s

our particular attention, as it comprehends within itſelf advantages which are of great value to the delicate invalid, and to
obtain which in almoſt any other part of England, he would
require to make a conſiderable journey."

The Undercliff. reminds one of nothing ſo much as of
one of Guſtave Doré's craggy panoramas.   Mantell thus
deſcribes this work of nature :—" The Undercliff may be
geologically deſcribed as a miſcellaneous débris, principally
compoſed of the fallen maſſes of the upper cretaceous ſtrata,
occaſioned by the encroachment of the ſea on the lower
argillaceous and ſandy depoſits that form the baſe of this
line of the coaſt.   It conſiſts of an irregular terrace, ſloping
towards the ſouth, from a quarter to half-a mile in breadth.
There is perhaps no tract of ſuch limited extent that affords
ſo remarkable an inſtance of the modification of climate produced by geological ſtructure and phyſical configuration, as
the Undercliff.   Of all the wonderful points along the Undercliff, the landſlip between Luccombe and Bonchurch is the
moſt ſtriking."

In comparatively recent years there have been two convul-
ſions of the land, which have modified the landſlip as we find
it.   The firſt took place in 1810, when twenty acres of land
were broken up and thrown down ; the ſecond in 1818, when
thirty acres were loſt.   Again, in 1847, a maſs of land fell.
The broken rocks, in their ſtillneſs, are fearful evidences of
the craſh which placed them where they are found.   Bruſh-
wood, ferns, wild flowers, lichens, and moſs, have covered the
ſcene with a lovely garment, but the craſh and war of the
falling rocks have left their mark upon the land.   The young
trees lift up their ſlender branches, and lo! in the courſe of
time the leaves touch ſome overhanging rock, arreſted as it
toppled, and which in ſome future ſlip muſt fall and ſhatter

them. Art and engineering may do much to prevent successive land slips in this part, but they cannot be wholly guarded against. Fortunately, the earth does not break up and melt as it were, without a fair warning.

The Rev. James White says of the Undercliff:—"It is a region so well known as hardly to require description. Consisting of a platform varying from half-a-mile to a quarter of a mile in width—bounded on the south by the undulating bays and promontories of the Channel, and on the north by a perpendicular wall of grey rocks, which forms the buttress to a range of downs of almost mountainous elevation, it is easy to perceive that it unites two of the principal constituents of a beautiful landscape. But when, besides its guardian hills and ever-varying ocean, we remember the richness of its vegetation, the clearness of its air, and the wild seclusion of its innumerable dells, the glowing expressions of enthusiastic tourists would seem not much, if at all, beyond the truth."

Wonderful Mrs. Radcliffe, the inventor of the "Mysteries of Udolpho," found the scenery of the Undercliff indeed sympathetic. She says:—"The Undercliff is a tract of shore formed by the fallen cliffs, and closely barricaded by a wall of rock of vast height. We entered upon it about a mile from Niton, and found ourselves in such a Druid scene of wildness and ruin as we never saw before. The road is, for the most part, close to the wall of rock, which seems to threaten the traveller with destruction, as he passes frequently beneath enormous masses that lean forward. On the other side of the road is an extremely rugged descent of about half-a-mile to the sea, where sometimes are amphitheatres of rocks, their theatres filled with ruins, and frequently covered with verdure and underwood that stretch up the hill-side with the wildest pomp, sheltering here a cottage and there a villa among the rocky hillocks. We afterwards afcended by a fteep rugged road to the fummit of the down, from which the views are aftonifhing and grand in a high degree ; we feemed perched on an extreme point of the world, looking down on hills and cliffs of various height and form, tumbled into confufion as if by an earthquake, and ftretching into the fea, which fpreads its vaft circumference beyond. The look down on the fhore is indeed tremendous."

Thorne, fpeaking of the geology of the Undercliff, remarks : "The ftrata, reckoning from the bottom, are firft red ferruginous fand, then blue marl, next green fandftone, and at the top chalk and chalk marl. The ftratum of blue marl is foft and eafily acted upon by land fprings, when it becomes mud, and oozes out; and the fandftone and chalk being deprived of their fupport, muft of neceffity fink down. The fubfidence, thus brought about, might be gradual and fcarcely perceptible, except in its ultimate refults; but the fea was at the fame time beating with violence againft the lower ftrata, and wafhing out the fand and marl, which were already loofened by the fprings. This double procefs would go on until the fuperincumbent mafs became unable to fuftain itfelf by mere adhefion to the parent rock, when it muft neceffarily break away and fall forward. That this was the way in which the Undercliff was produced, is evident from an examination of the phenomena it prefents, and what may be obferved ftill going on, though on a leffer fcale. The great change in the level muft have occurred at a very diftant period; churches and houfes of ancient date, which ftand in different parts of the Undercliff, fhow that no very confiderable alteration can have taken place for centuries."

"I have counted," fays Dr. Martin, "nearly fifty fpecies of garden flowers blooming in the Undercliff gardens in December."

BONCHURCH

Bonchurch.

ONCHURCH is eſſentially the Swiſs bit of the
iſland. One almoſt expects to hear the Ranz
des Vaches ſuddenly mingling with the ſheep
bells on the down. The pool reminds one of
a nook of a Swiſs lake a—châlet only is wanting
to complete the ſcene.

But Bonchurch has a higher claim to our
regards than its mere beauty. If tradition is
right, it was at Bonchurch that the firſt Chriſtian
miſſionaries landed with their meſſage of peace
and good-will. If this were ſo, the place is in
our day moſt felicitouſly named. Bonchurch, it
is ſaid, is a corruption of *bonecerce;* and the
aſſociation of the words appears very admiſſible. The miſſion-
ary who landed in the Iſle of Wight was St. Boniface. Even
to this day there is a tiny cove amongſt the rocks ſtyled Monk's
Bay. It is ſaid that this name has adhered to it ſince A.D. 755,
when ſome adventurous Chriſtian monks of the Abbey of Lire
ſet their feet on Britiſh ground.

Bonchurch pariſh church is very old, but of courſe it lays no

claim to fo extraordinary an antiquity as the eftablifhment of
Chriftianity in the ifland. It is fuppofed it was founded by a
De Lisle about the commencement of the fourteenth century.
It is not a very rich living—£134 per annum.

Bonchurch contains within its limits a greater variety of
fcenery than is to be found anywhere elfe in a fimilar expanfe
over the whole ifland. The fublime and the picturefque are
combined here in the moft ftriking manner. Here is an
immenfe wall of chalk—at its foot a crowded dell of flowers.
On this fide is the flope of a fward dipping to the beach; on the
other the fteep afcent of St. Boniface Down. The entrance to
the village, whether from eaft or weft, is beyond defcription
moft lovely, and if the vifit be well-timed, the furface of the
Bonchurch pool will be dotted with the broad leaves and white
flowers of the water lily. But whatever bit of fcenery the eye
falls on, the leaft turn prefents the friendly towering cliff-wall
—the winter ftore, fo to fpeak, of the Undercliff. Here the
cliff varies from four to five hundred feet in height, broken
delightfully in places by the grounds of charming villas, where
art has aided nature to produce a perfect refult.

And as St. Boniface Down is fo very high (783 feet above
the fea), of courfe the tourift will fcale it if only to reach
the celebrated well, called St. Bonny's Well, a perpetual fpring
which bubbles clear and cold from the white depths of the
chalky down. In the ifland they attribute the difcovery of this
well to a grotefque fort of miracle. A certain bifhop, name and
fee unknown, being on a mifty night travelling on the fummit of
the down, though why and wherefore are queftions to which the
legend has no reply, fuddenly found his fteed flipping down the
precipice. The horfe and his rider were temporarily faved by
being caught in the hollow in which this well is to be found.
The bifhop now vows to St. Boniface, the patron faint of the

place, that if he reaches level ground alive he will dedicate an acre of land in his honour. Apparently St. Boniface, with that good nature which has made him the patron faint of all innkeepers, heard the promife, for that the bifhop got down in fafety is fufficiently proved by the fact that there is a Bifhop's Acre ftill forming part of the glebe of Bonchurch. It is to be feen at the bottom of the hill.

This well in the middle ages was the climax of a fort of flower pilgrimage. On the feaft of St. Boniface, the maidens would bring here votive offerings of the abundant flowers growing in the valley below. And to this day there are people in Bonchurch who believe that whatever you wifh, if you keep it a fecret when you firft drink of the water of the well, is certain to come to pafs.

The view from the fummit of St. Boniface Down is a panorama of perfect harmony—the far-off fea alive with the reflection of the fleecy clouds, a fhifting embroidery of fhadow, light, and colour, totally beyond the power of defcription.

Near the pool the wanderer will find a flight of fteps which leads to the Pulpit Rock, a broken mafs of cliff 400 feet above the level of the fea. And now coming down paft the pool, which is fed by a ftream that rifes from the down, and runs off underground in two directions, we turn our faces towards Ventnor, not without fome friendly glances towards the vil- lagers of Bonchurch, who are perhaps as pleafant a fet as you fhall meet within the ifle; and it muft be confeffed that the unceafing paffage of tourifts (a percentage of whom, here as everywhere elfe, are not fufficiently felf-refpecting to know their duty to their neighbours), has not tended to make the iflanders more than neceffarily courteous. However, even a Frenchman was, fome two fcore years fince, edified by the courtefy of the people of the ifland.

M. Louis Simonds, in his journal of a tour and refidence in
Great Britain, fpeaks rapturoufly of the politenefs, neatnefs, and
love of order, fhown by the villagers of the Ifle of Wight:—
"The meaneft of the cottages," he fays, "are adorned with
rofes, jeffamines, and honey-fuckles, and often large myrtles.
There are vines everywhere againft their houfes, and often fig
trees.   We thought the women remarkably good looking.
Children and grown people took of their hats or gave us a nod
as we paffed along."

VENTNOR

Ventnor.

HE rife of Ventnor is one of the moft magica
facts in the hiftory of the Ifle of Wight. In
comparatively recent guides to the ifle the
name does not occur. There is to be found
Ventnor Cove, but no Ventnor. It was
fimply a fmall fifhing village, beneath the
notice of the mappift.

Sixty years fince the Crab and Lobfter
tavern, the New Inn, and three or four
fifhermen's huts, made up Ventnor. It is
of courfe, now one of the leading towns in
the ifle; perhaps, taken all the year round, it is the moft
flourifhing. And yet it has no hiftory. It is the metropolis of
the Undercliff, and has overwhelmed Bonchurch and converted it into a fuburb. But even now it is not a parifh in
itfelf, being a parochial outfkirt of Newchurch. The only
fragment of antiquity about Ventnor is the derivation of its
name. Antiquarians with a Celtic turn of mind, deduce this
from *gwent*, chalky, and *nor*, fhore. But this is juft one of
thofe queftions which are never quite fettled.

T

It was Sir James Clark who raifed Ventnor from a village
to a town. Had the doctor been as clever a commercial man
as a phyfician, he would have bought fome acres of Ventnor
before he gave it an exiftence. His defcendants, fhould any
exift, would at this moment be rich in ground rents.

Knight, fpeaking of this fudden rife in the deftinies of the
town, fays:—"Forty years ago it contained about half a dozen
humble cottages; and until the publication of Sir James Clark's
work its few inhabitants were nearly all fifhermen. It was
the moft picturefque fpot along the coaft. The platform was
broken into feveral uneven terraces. The huge hills towered
far up aloft. Down to the broad fmooth beach the ground ran
in rough flopes, mingled with abrupt banks of rock, along which
a brawling rivulet careered gaily towards the fea; and the few
fifhermen's huts gave a piquant ruftic livelinefs to all befides.
The climate feemed moft favourable, and the neighbourhood
moft agreeable to the invalid. In the open gardens of the cot-
tagers, myrtle and other tender plants flourifhed abundantly, and
without need of protection even in winter; fnow hardly ever
lay on the ground ; funny and fheltered walks abounded ; and
the beach was excellent for bathing. Ventnor at once caught
the attention of the crowd of vifitors; and it was one of the
firft places to provide them fuitable accommodation. In the
tiny fifhing hamlet foon fprang up hotels, and boarding-houfes,
and fhops, and a church. Invalids came here for a winter
retreat, as well as a fummer vifit. Speculation was ftimulated.
And now, as Fuller has it, 'the plague of building lighted upon
it,' and it fpread until every poffible fpot was planted with fome
ftaring building, or row of buildings."

Sir James Clark fays of the Ventnor diftrict: "It was a matter
of furprife to him, after having fully examined that favoured
fpot, that the advantages it poffeffed in fo eminent a degree, in

point of fhelter and pofition, fhould have been fo long overlooked in a country like this, whofe inhabitants during the laft
century have been traverfing half the globe in fearch of climate.
The phyfical ftructure of this fingular diftrict has been carefully inveftigated and defcribed by the geologift, and the beauties
of its fcenery have been often dwelt upon by the tourift ; but
its far more important qualities as a winter refidence for the
delicate invalid feem fcarcely to have attracted attention, even
from the medical philofopher. Nothing," he continues, " along
the fouth coaft will bear a comparifon with it, and Torquay is
the only place on the fouth-weft coaft which will do fo. With
a temperature nearly the fame, the climate of Torquay will be
found fofter, more humid, and relaxing ; while that of the
Undercliff will prove drier, fomewhat fharper, and more
bracing."

Ventnor is municipally governed by a Board of Commis-
fioners, who in their time have built the fea wall and contrived
an efplanade. From the fea the town has a wonderful charm
for us, but it is only fair to add, that moft writers complain
bitterly of its general afpect. One of the more recent authorities fays :—" We may obferve, *en paffant*, that in no town in
England have builders indulged fuch monftrous vagaries as in
this. There is fcarcely a villa of modeft or unpretending
afpect in the whole town ; and to pafs through its ftreets is
enough to affect a fenfitive architect with a hideous nightmare !"
But, for our part, we maintain that the accidental nature of the
ftreet architecture of Ventnor is one of its charms.

And is this all that can be faid of Ventnor ? No—on the
beach may be now and again found very clear cryftal pebbles.
Thefe are Ventnor diamonds. But the truer diamonds are the
brightened eyes which are beftowed upon the invalids by the
health-giving powers of this town. During the paft fummer

(1868) an impreffion drifted abroad that Ventnor, from its
enclofed fituation, was fuffering fearfully from that heat which
diftinguifhed the feafon. On the contrary, in the height of
fummer it appears to exhibit the meteorological phenomenon
of falling below the average temperature of the ifland as the
thermometer rifes.

A perfon of much authority writing on this fubject, fays :—
"During the exceffively hot weather of July and Auguft, 1868,
the temperature here was many degrees lower than in the
majority of places in other parts of England, owing mainly to
the fea-breeze which, with the regularity of a trade wind, fets
in each afternoon, and to the cliffs, eaft and weft, giving fo
much fhade to the town. Thus whilft warm and fheltered in
winter, yet in fummer the climate here is cool and pleafant,
owing to the amount of fhade afforded by the locality. During
July the greateft out-of-door heat in fhade was 78 degrees, and
indoors 74 degrees, whilft upwards of 90 degrees was recorded
elfewhere."

It is in winter however, that Ventnor becomes a kind of
earthly paradife to the invalid, fo fheltered is it by the hills
around. Thefe hills then appear to have fome power of
arrefting the heat of the foutherly and wefterly winds, and radia-
ting it back upon Ventnor, fo that when on the other and
northern flope of the downs a froft has fet in, in Ventnor
itfelf bees are to be feen buzzing from one to another of two
fcore varieties of flowers.

A fpot with fuch qualifications as thefe requires no hiftory :
it fpeaks for itfelf.

*   *   *   *   *   *   *

Leaving Ventnor, the tourift fets out for St. Lawrence,
glancing at Ventnor Cove, as he leaves the town of undying
fummer behind him. In 1793, a traveller, who could fay

nothing of Ventnor (for it did not exift), had a few words to fay of the cove. The traveller was Wyndham; and he fays:— "The little cove of Ventnor is very well known for its romantic fcenery, and for a confiderable cafcade of fine water, which, after turning a corn-mill, falls upon the beach, as well as for its crab and lobfter fifhery, all of which are deftined for the London markets."

The tourift has to keep a very fharp look out for the little church of St. Lawrence—the fmalleft in the ifle certainly, and we believe the fmalleft parifh church in the United Kingdom. Being furrounded by trees, he may, if he takes the lower road, pafs the building without feeing it. The communion table, reading defk, pulpit, and pews, are all pufhed up together; and as there is no veftry, the minifter leaves his veftments on the communion rails between the fervices. In fummer time the tiny windows on the fouth fide, and the fouth door (the only one), are left open, and the church is ingenioufly enlarged by means of an awning and a few forms. It is to be regretted that fome years fince the incumbent felt himfelf under the necesfity of fetting up a board reproving tourifts, recommending them to keep holy the Sabbath, and requefting them not to interrupt the fervice. One feels that perhaps it were better that any interruption to the fervice fhould be patiently borne (a procefs which might lead the offender to a filent repentance at the end of a mile's walk), than that a feeling of anger fhould be created by this board, which is regularly brought out with fine weather. Time has dulled the pointed reproof, but it is ftill demonftrative enough to jarr with the beautiful landfcape, the murmur of prayer, and the fweet ferenity which pervades the fpot when the quaint half open-air fervice is progreffing.

The church is barely fix feet to the eaves, and it it is only twenty-five feet four inches long, by eleven feet broad; and, indeed, before the *enlargement*, by the late Earl of Yarborough, it was only twenty feet long.

One John Green, of St. Lawrence, who flourifhed in 1835, was moved to poetic expreffion over the minutenefs of this parifh church. Excufing ourfelves for the act, we offer a copy of thefe verfes.

ON ST. LAWRENCE CHURCH;
Being the fmalleft in the Britifh Dominions.

"This Church has often drawn the curious eye,
    To fee its length and breadth, to fee how high;
At length to meafure it, 'twas my intent,
    That I might certify its full extent.
Its breadth from fide to fide, above the bench,
    Is juft eleven feet and half an inch;
Its height from pavement to the ceiling mortar,
    Eleven feet, four inches, and a quarter;
And its length from Eaft to the Weft end,
    I tell the truth to you, you may depend;
Twenty-five feet, four inches, quarters three,
    Is juft its meafurement as you may fee.
And fituated clofe to the high road,
    Here you may join in pray'r, and worfhip God;
And though the building is fo low and fmall,
    You may be near to heaven, as at St. Paul.
It ftands firm on fome confecrated ground,
    Fenc'd with a wall, and ivy growing round;
Its length is fixty feet, breadth forty-two,
    And there the dead do meet to wait for you."

Leaving St. Lawrence, we are fairly on our way to Blackgang Chine, and the effect produced by that defolate example of nature, if we may be permitted the expreffion, is enhanced by the walk between St. Lawrence and Chale. No pen—not even that of Rufkin, or of the poet whofe refidence we are nearing—that of Tennyfon—could adequately defcribe the marvellous charm of the mingled paftoral and grand which here reigns in perfection. On the one hand breaks of graffy flopes leading to the fea; on the other the undulating line of the cliff, piled up in a fort of mockery, as it were, of the builder's art. One moment the fea is ftretched before you, the next it is hidden by a fweep of trees, or luxurious garden. A turn to the right, and you are brought abreaft of the cliff; another turn in the road, and the cliff is behind you, and the fea is feen between two large clumps of beech. The ivy here is a tapeftry, fpreading over ground, trees, hedges, the very cliff itfelf revelling in its favoured growth. Suddenly another turn in the road, and you are bathed in a tender toned fhadow. Looking up you find that it is due to fome meeting beech trees, the tranfparent leaves of which offer the moft exquifite paffage for light in the whole range of the world of leaves; and fo the tourift paffes Old Park and Mirables, (the latter well named), and comes out by St. Catherine's Lighthoufe. And here the Undercliff opens out once again into a wild and broken panorama, ending in the great wafte and frowning mafs called Blackgang.

Blackgang Chine.

———

TO our thinking, nothing in all Englifh fcenery is fo ghaftly and horror-infpiring as this place. It is the more fearful that it is in juxta-pofition to fo many natural beauties. The very fancy bazaar through which the fcene is reached, the ftalls of foffils and rock fpecimens tended by a fmiling girl, all the vulgar evidences of the anticipation of vifitors, but aid in promoting the feeling of defolation which comes upon the fpectator when he has left humanity behind him and is alone. Not a tree or fhrub tames the primeval favagery of this place. Adown in the bafin the wanderer finds one or two fcattered ferns, and he welcomes them as friends. The effect of the Blackgang—a term faid to be derived from the tone of its general colour, and *gang*, a way (the black road)—and its favage defolation, cannot be experienced if viewed in company: one muft be alone—not during moonlight, for moonlight poeticifes the chafm, but at twilight or day-break, when the

BLACKGANG CHINE.

fhadows lie long and pointed over the filent wafte. Within
its grafp it has not one redeeming feature of beauty, not one
lovely line nor foft undulation. All is dank, dark, human-
lcfs. And this is how the world appeared before vegetation
arofe, when no life was on the land, and light had but commenced its vivifying work. One remembers the fuggeftions of
life and humanity at Shanklin, and is glad to get away from the
fcene; rifing above it upon the return walk, a fenfe of relief is
experienced. It is to us a caufe for marvelling that tourifts,
notably brides and bridegrooms, can remain a whole honeymoon
in the prefence of this abomination of defolation. It is a fight
worth feeing, but not one which the tourift, as a rule, wifhes
to witnefs a fecond time.

　　"Ah, fir," fays a pleafant old woman, "you fhould have
feen the Blackgang when *I* was a girl. It was then worth
feeing. It tumbled in when I was a young maid, an' there
be nothing left of it now." Nothing left of it! Then what
muft it have once been?

　　The date of the laft great downfall of the Blackgang is
not known with precifion, for at that time it was not the
lion it has fince become, and the neighbouring Ventnor had
not fprung into exiftence. But there can be little hefitation in
fixing it at about 1799, for in that year a very remarkable land-
flip occurred in the land lying behind it, the effect of which
muft have been felt by the tottering maffes of the Blackgang.
The fubfidence occurred at a farm called Pitlands, lying on the
boundary line between Chale and Niton. An area of 100
acres was obferved to be in motion, and continued fo during
two fucceffive days, directing its courfe towards the fea in
nearly a direct line. The changes which took place upon the
furface were extremely curious, as there was fcarcely a fquare
yard but altered its appearance, both rocks and trees fhifting

their fituations, and forming as confufed a fcene as if the ground
had been convulfed by an earthquake. In many places the
earth funk to the depth of thirty or forty feet; and a cottage
which had been taftefully fitted up as a profpect houfe, was
partly thrown down and buried in the fiffures; the ground
then began to move, and the lands of the farm, being preffed
on by the defcending mafs, were torn from their original foundations, and fuddenly moved forward till all further progrefs
was ftopped by the ftability of a ridge of rocks, which, like an
oppofing barrier, prevented the wreck from rufhing headlong
into the fea.

In 1810-11, the year of the great landflips between Shanklin
and Bonchurch, another fubfidence took place ; and again,
about twenty years fince, a flip of country, about a mile fouth
of Niton, moved fufficiently to give the idea of land which had
been convulfed by an earthquake. A houfe was engulfed by
that cataftrophe.

Obferved from the fea, much of the defolation of the Blackgang departs, atmofphere no doubt tending to ameliorate its
afpect. Mantell, the geologift of the ifland, thus fpeaks of the
chine under thefe circumftances:—

" Viewed from the fea at low water, efpecially when the fprings
which feed the waterfall have been fwollen by heavy rains, the
effect is highly picturefque. The cafcade falls in a perpendicular column from a ledge feventy feet high, down the midft
of a deep chafm, formed in dark ferruginous clays and fands,
and furmounted by broken cliffs 400 feet high, and towering
above all is the majeftic efcarpment of St. Catherine's Hill,
rifing to an altitude of between 800 and 900 feet. The bands
of greenifh-grey fand and fandftone, which alternate with ferruginous clays in this divifion of the green-fand fyftem, appear
very prominent, owing to the wearing away of the foft and

friable intermediate beds. As the face of the fandftone after long expofure to the atmofphere feparates into fquare blocks, the appearance of the projecting bands of ftone, which are from ten to fifteen feet thick, is very fingular, and is not inaptly compared by Sir Henry Englefield to courfes of mafonry built up at different heights to fuftain the mouldering cliffs. The thin layer of ironftone grit which is very conftantly found in this divifion of the green-fand, conftituting as it were a line of demarcation between the upper arenaceous depofis and the lower more argillaceous group, intercepts the water that per-colates through the upper porous ftrata, and projecting in a ledge forms the bed of the ftream that falls in a cafcade over the face of the cliff."

Wyndham, an earlier writer, gives a very profaic account of the Blackgang. " The chine is on the weft declivity of St. Catherine's Hill (769 feet), and its upper appearance is not far below its high fummit; two currents, from diftant parts of this hill, have made their way to its brow, and from this height have excavated two large feparate chafms, but their waters form a junction at the bafe of a high prominent point, the fides of which have been worn away by the refpective torrents. The chafms at this point become one, and confequently much deepened; from whence the united waters more rapidly hurry down the fteep channel for about 200 yards, till they arrive at an im-penetrable precipice of rock (a layer of ironftone grit), from whence they fall in a perpendicular cafcade of 70 feet upon the fhore."

The Blackgang however, has its romance. Pennant fays :— " The country people in thefe parts once thought that they were poffeffed of a Pactolian fand, for they obtained for a certain time fome gold duft from the fand of the bay; but, from a number of dollars having been from time to time caft on

fhore, it was juftly fufpected that it came from the wreck of
fome unfortunate Spanifh fhip."

Not the only veffel to break up hereabouts was the Spanifh
galleon. Chale churchyard is a mute record of the going down
of men into the fea; and under thefe cliffs, on October 11th,
1836, the good fhip *Clarendon* was loft. Of a crew of feven-
teen, together with eleven paffengers, all except three were
drowned.

Up, out of the chine, and fo through the bazaar, where the
only appropriate object to be found is the fkeleton of an enormous whale, alfo wrecked in this neighbourhood.

Leaving the filent pafs, it is well to go up upon St. Catherine's
Hill, the highelt ground in the ifland. On the fummit of
this noble mount are the towers which form a fplendid landmark. The wind is never at peace at the top of St. Catherine's, fo named becaufe of a hermitage founded there in the
fourteenth century, and dedicated to St. Catherine as the
patronefs faint of all high elevations. In the regifters of Winchefter reference will be found to this windy hermitage—no
fpot for a felf-indulgent hermit. Thus runs the regiftration:—
" Walter de Langftrell, admiffus ad hermitorium fupra montem
de Chale, in infula Vectis, idib. Octobris, A.D. 1312." "Walter de Langftrell, admitted to the hermitage at the fummit of
Chale mount, in the Ifle of Wight."

Worfley, fpeaking of what happened when the fite was
cleared for the erection of a new landmark, fays:—"The foundation of the whole chapel was alfo cleared and levelled; by
which, not only its figure was difcovered, but alfo the floor and
ftone hearth of the prieft's little cell at the fouth-weft corner."

Mantell has alfo fomething to fay of St. Catherine's:—" It is
the weftern extremity of the fouthern range of chalk downs,
which is feparated by a confiderable diftrict of green-fand from

the central chain of hills. This fyſtem of chalk downs varies in
breadth from half-a-mile to three miles, and extends ſix miles
in a direction E.N.E and W.S.W., from St. Catherine's Hill
to Dunnofe, its eaſtern termination, which is 771 feet high.
The intermediate parts of this range maintain an elevation of
from 650 to 800 feet, with the exception of a deep valley on
the eaſt of St. Catherine's, through which the road to Niton
paſſes, and another at Steep Hill, called the Shute, or Shoot,
above Ventnor, traverſed by the road to Appuldurcombe and
Newport."

Cook, in his "New Picture of the Iſle of Wight," ſays,
"Sometimes, in the cleareſt weather, may be ſeen even the
higheſt part of the French coaſt, adjoining Cherbourg; but
this is rare, to the fight even of the party ſtationed at the
Signal Houſe." We however, doubt this ſtatement.

And now we defcend to the head of the Blackgang once
again. The appearance of this ſpot, with its bazaar and
attendants, differs ſtrangely from a defcription of it ſixty years
ago, which runs as follows:—"Here, on the higheſt ſide of
the dreadful precipice, on a narrow ledge of land not many yards
from the fartheſt projection of the rock, that defcends perpen-
dicularly near 500 feet, is the hut of a ſhepherd, whoſe family
braves the conflicting elements in the moſt dreadful feaſons.

"The chine may, with ſome little trouble, be defcended,
following the progrefs of the ſtream as it makes its way to the
beach below. This will be neceſſary in order to enjoy the
two grand views that the chine affords. Thoſe who cannot
take the trouble, will however, by defcending but a little dis-
tance, have ſome idea of the upper view, from which, among
an uncommon difplay of rugged ſcenery and impending crags,
they will enjoy outwards a fine profpect extending to the
Needles.

" The cliff being of a fofter quality lower down, its trickling
inwards, and occafional dafhing over fome jutting pieces of
rock, has hollowed a cavity fome yards within the falling ftream ;
fo that we may ftand infide, and looking through the fhower
that falls without, admire its prifmatic colours when oppofed to
the fun's rays, or receive its gentle dropping on our heads, a
natural fhower bath.

" This cavern has a folemn and an almoft awful afpect,
having the black mineral-like appearance that pervades the
cliffs above. The ftrata have the refemblance of an afcent
of gigantic fteps, whence, probably, and from its frowning
afpect, it derives its name. An adjoining chine, of much
inferior magnitude, is known by the name of *Ladder Chine*,
from the fame appearance of the ftrata which characterifes the
cliffs of Chale Bay for a confiderable extent."

CARISBROOK CASTLE.

Carifbrook and its Caftle.

———◦———

"I DO not think," wrote Keats, "I fhall ever fee a ruin to furpafs Carifbrook Caftle. The trench is overgrown with the fmootheft turf, and the walls with ivy. The keep withinfide is one bower of ivy; a colony of jackdaws has been there for many years. I dare fay I have feen many a defcendant of fome old cawer who peeped through the bars at Charles I., when he was there in confinement."

Carifbrook Caftle has done its work. There is no longer any need for the protection of frowning and armed mountain of ftones; and therefore old caftles are all crumbling to decay—beautiful, folemn, peaceful, filent, and dead.

Carifbrook poffeffes for the hiftorian the great charm of being the laft feudal ftronghold in which a ftruggle took place between the declining power of the few, and the rifing power of the many, for it was here the rafh, if brave, Charles Stuart threw his laft ftake, and loft.

Carifbrook is about a mile and-a-half from Newport, and is
fituated upon a peculiarly round hill—a *glacis* in itfelf, fuch a
one as may have given the idea of the artificial defence to the
foldier who firft brought it into practical ufe. The general
appearance as feen from the road, is ftrikingly picturefque. The
ftrong outline of its ruined wall and towering keep, the abrupt
fweep down towards the valley, the whole backed by Bowcombe
Downs, yield a maffive panorama.

The origin of the caftle is traced to the Saxons. But we
doubt much if this decifion is to be admitted. If Newport
really does prefent all the evidences in its outlines of a large
Roman town, it is evident that a Roman camp could not have
been far away. And as a Roman camp was always fixed upon
a hill when that pofition was practicable, and the hill upon
which Carifbrook ftands was well fituated, anfwered all the
conditions required by a Roman general, and was within twenty
javelins' caft of Newport, it is probable that a Roman camp
was the firft fhape of fortification which was built here—if,
indeed, fuch a camp was not preceded by Celtic entrenchments.

The fuppofition, in reference to a Roman camp, is to
fome extent ftrengthened by the recent difcovery of a tes-
felated Roman pavement in the grounds of Carifbrook parfonage. Some workmen were digging here in 1858, when
their labours led to the difcovery of the pavement in queftion.
Antiquarians were foon on the fpot, and the evident remains of
a Roman villa at once were perceived. The Romans knew
how to choofe fites. A hill fheltered the rear of the villa,
before it lay the valley of the Medina, while the protective
camp on the fummit of the hill of Carifbrook, guaranteed it
from the danger of a fudden enemy failing up the river. The
villa—by its fize—muft have belonged to a perfon of the
very higheft diftinction. The teffelated pavement, open

once more to the light, is very beautiful, and ftill retains much
of the brilliancy of its original colouring. Her Majefty the
Queen, upon her frequent vifits to Carifbrook, which take
place generally with members of the royal family, but fometimes with vifitors to Ofborne, has on feveral occafions in
fpeéted this pavement, while during one vifit the royal pencil
was occupied for fome time in making a drawing of this remarkable evidence of Roman fupremacy.

The Rev. Edward Kell, M.A., has devoted much time and
critical acumen to prove that the Roman occupation of the Ifle
of Wight was important and long continued. The difcovery
of the Carifbrook Roman pavement, fix years after this gentleman had publifhed his impreffions, helped confiderably to fub-
ftantiate his views in conneétion with the Roman fway in
Wight. Mr. Kell maintains his belief not only upon the
evidence of coins of the conformation of Newport, but upon
the ftill exifting names of ftreets in that town. For inftance,
he urges that Pyle Street is the corruption of pylum, a gate, or
port. Within the paft hundred years Pyle Street was the one
way out of Newport towards Ryde, by means of the ford
at the bottom of that ftreet. Mr. Kell maintains, obfcurely
however, that Lugley Street is from lux ; while Crocker Street
reminds him of crocus—yellow. Much more rational is his
argument to the effeét that Scarrot's Lane is from *fcarrofus*,
rough.

The exifting architeéture of the caftle may be divided into
three diftinét periods. The firft is Saxon, and includes part
of the keep containing fragments which it has been demonftrated muft be of 1,200 years antiquity. To this fucceeds the
architeéture of the Norman Conqueft, about which time the
area of the caftle appears to have been much extended. The final
period is referable to the reign of Elizabeth, when in anticipa-

tion of the inimical pofition Spain was evidently about to take up, all the lateft advances in fortification and defence were rapidly applied to this important ftronghold. Thefe additions chiefly took the fhape of outworks, and modifications of the outer angles of the walls, and refulted in bringing the circum-ference of the fortrefs up to three quarters of a mile, the whole enclofing an area of about twenty acres.

The tourift reaches Carifbrook Caftle from Newport by the Mall, and croffing the brook, which together with *caer*, a ftronghold, gives the name to the caftle, he is at liberty to afcend the fteep road which leads to it.

By the way, it was in this brook that a fcion of royalty a year or fo back took an unexpected bath. The Prince Arthur, accompanying other members of the royal family, was at this point, the interfection of the road and brook, thrown from his pony, fortunately to have his fall broken by a plafh in the fhallow water.

"And is there anything elfe remarkable about the brook?" we afk.

"Oh, yes," fays our informant, who, living fo near the great fhow place, Carifbrook, is neceffarily fomewhat in the nature of a guide—"Oh, yes, when there is rain the brook here where we ftand is worth feeing, for the water coming down from Carifbrook is chalky white, the rain from the road is yellow with gravel, and the brook comes down from the lake bright as before, and 'tis ftrange to fee how they battle before they mix."

Reaching the gateway, having got paft the pickets in the way of greedy pioneers and boys with horrid gritty landfcapes, made from the beautiful fands of Alum Bay, the tourift finds himfelf under the fhadow of the gateway of Elizabeth's time. The guide-books tell you that you can fee the letters

E. R., and the date 1598 on the outer walls. Recent years
have fretted thefe evidences from the face of the building.
Now crofling the ftone bridge which fpans the moat—a rare
expanfe of which the flora of Wight avails itfelf to luxuriate
at pleafure, we reach a heavy gateway, grooved for portcullis,
and clofed with the ancient iron-ftudded gates, now haftening
faft to decay. The tourift may have read that the efcutcheon
of the Woodville family is to be feen over the gateway.
Certainly it requires good eyes to fee this heraldry. The
efcutcheon and the white rofe of the houfe of York, once
carved on thefe walls, have long fince been peeled by froft and
time from the furface of the ftone.

An echoing knock brings a well-dreffed janitor to the door,
who admits you filently to the interior of the building. To the
left, and up a few broken fteps, you find what was once a
fuite of apartments. There are ftill the remains of fire-
places and chimneys, which might be put to ufe. They long
fince grew cold. Thefe crumbling ftones are all that remain
of the rooms in which Charles I. paffed fome of the bitter
months which preceded his more bitter end. The guide points
out a window as that from which the king tried to efcape.
Hillier however, maintains that the true window " was blocked
up in after alterations, but is neverthelefs eafily recognifable on
the exterior of the wall, looking from the moat, as it nearly
adjoins the only buttrefs on that fide of the caftle."

The hiftory of Charles Stuart is told by Gilpin. He fays :—
"Colonel Hammond, into whofe power Charles threw himfelf,
was then governor of the Ifle of Wight. He feems to have
been a man of humanity,* and while his hands were untied to

---

* One authority however, ftates that Hammond was prepared to fhoot the king
while trying to efcape, had Charles fucceeded in paffing the window of his dungeon.

have been difpofed to fhow the king every civility in his power. Charles took his exercife on horfe-back where he pleafed, though his motions were probably obferved ; and as the Parliament had granted him £5,000 a year, he lived for a few months in fomething like royal ftate.

" But this liberty was very foon abridged. His chaplains and fervants were firft taken from him ; then his going abroad in the ifland gave offence ; and foon after his intercourfe with anybody but thofe fet about him was checked. So folitary was his confinement, during a greater part of this time, that as he was ftanding one day near the gate of the caftle with Sir Philip Warwick, he pointed to an old decrepit man walking acrofs one of the courts, and faid, 'That man is fent every morning to light my fire, and he is the beft companion I have had for many months.'

"All this fevere ill-ufage Charles bore with patience and equanimity, and endeavoured as much as poffible, to keep his mind employed. He had ever been impreffed with ferious thoughts of religion, which his misfortunes had now ftrengthened and confirmed. Devotion, meditation, and ftudy of the Scriptures, were his great confolation. The few books he had brought with him to the caftle were chiefly on religious fubjects, or of a ferious caft. Among them was ' Hooker's Ecclefiaftical Polity.' This book, it is probable, he had ftudied with great attention, as it related much to the national queftion of that time, in which no man was better verfed. In his flender catalogue we find alfo two books of amufement : Taffo's ' Jerufalem,' and Spenfer's ' Faery Queen.'

" His exercife was now much abridged. As horfe exercife was refufed, he fpent two or three hours every morning in walking on the caftle ramparts. Here he enjoyed at leaft a fine air, and an extenfive profpect ; though every object he faw, the flocks ſtraying careleſſly on one ſide, and the ſhips ſailing freely on the other, put him in mind of that liberty of which he was ſo cruelly deprived.   In the mean time, he was totally careleſs of his perſon; he let his beard and hair grow, and was inattentive to his dreſs.

"During the time of his impriſonment in Cariſbrook Caſtle, three attempts were made, chiefly by the gentlemen of the iſland, to reſcue him.   Lord Clarendon gives us the detail of two of them; but a third, which he had heard of, he ſuppoſes to be a mere fiction.   As it is mentioned however, in the Worſley papers, with every mark of authenticity, and as one of the principal conductors of it was a gentleman of that family, there ſeems to be little doubt of its being a fact.   The following is an abſtract of it:—

"By a correſpondence privately ſettled with ſome gentlemen in the iſland, it was agreed, that the king ſhould let himſelf down by a cord from a window of his apartment.   A ſwift horſe with a guide, was to wait for him at the bottom of the ramparts; and a veſſel in the offing was to be ready to convey him where he pleaſed.   The chief difficulty was how the king ſhould get through the iron bars of his window.   But Charles aſſured them he had tried the paſſage, and did not doubt but it was ſufficiently large.   But on the ſign being given, and the king beginning the attempt, he ſoon found he had made a falſe calculation.   Having protruded his head and ſhoulders, he could get no farther; and what was worſe, he could not draw himſelf back.   His friends at the bottom heard him groan in his dis-treſs, but were unable to relieve him.   At length however, by repeated efforts, he got himſelf diſengaged; but made at that time no further attempt.   Afterwards he contrived to ſaw the bars of his window aſunder: and another ſcheme was laid; but the particulars of this Lord Clarendon details.

" The treaty of Newport foon after followed ; after which
Charles was feized by the army, and carried a prifoner to Hurft
Caftle. In his way thither he met Mr. Worfley, one of the
gentlemen who rifked his life for him at Carifbrook. Charles
wrung his hand with affection, and pulling his watch out of his
pocket, gave it to him, faying, ' That is all my gratitude has to
give.'

" This watch is ftill preferved in the family. It is of filver,
large and clumfy in its form. The cafe is neatly ornamented
with filigree; but the movements are of very ordinary workman-
fhip, and wound up with catgut."

To return to the caftle. On the right upon entering may
be feen the ruins of a chapel dedicated to St. Nicholas, built
during the laft century upon the fite of the original chapel
founded by Fitz-Ofbert.

The *Bowling Green*, or *Tilt Yard*, which now comes into
view, was conftructed by Hammond for the ufe of the imprifoned King. This bowling green is as perfect at this moment
as though it had only been laid down a year or two fince ; as
perfect as when Charles played upon it ; as when his daughter
Elizabeth, who delighted in bowls, rolled her laft bowl over
the fmooth grafs.

Before the tourift, as he enters the caftle yard, are the
governor's apartments, of which the following account is
given in the *Builder :*—" The plain, indeed the fomewhat
ugly manfion which faces you as you enter, appears to have
been modernised out of the original *Hall*, and divided into two
ftories. It was formerly connected with the keep by a ftrong
wall. During the recent repairs—ably directed by Mr. Hard-
wicke, the architect—many interefting details, hitherto concealed, have been difcovered. A ftalwart chimney, and one of
the ancient windows on the fide oppofite to the keep, may now

be feen. The *fmaller* of the *two* chapels which once exifted within the caftle precincts—the chapel erected by Ifabella de Fortibus—has been brought to light. The fide window remains, and the beautiful arcade on both fides, but of the eaft window there is no trace but the pofition of the fill; it is now occupied by the great ftaircafe which Lord Cutts put up when he repaired the governor's refidence."

And it is adjoining this modernifed manfion, where now live the cuftodians, and on the left, that the grandeft remains of the caftle are to be feen. The great room, probably once a banqueting hall, is vaft in fize, and here it is that Her Majefty takes a picnic tea when fhe vifits the place. The woodwork is ftill found, and the plafter being very white offers an irrefiftible temptation to tourifts to infcribe their names, which fwarm over the walls of this part of the caftle.

In one cafe however, a foreigner, with fome artiftic power, has drawn a coat-of-arms and a motto high upon the wall. The arms are compofed of a Maltefe crofs upon a curtain. The motto, *Un pour Tous—Tous pour Un.* Done heavily in crayon, the defign ftarts out upon the barenefs of the long melancholy room, with an intenfity which at once arrefts attention.

On another part of the wall may be found thefe lines:—

> "See how the mighty fhrink into a fong."—BYRON.

> " Ye who may ramble round thefe crumbling walls,
> See in what way grim ruin is appeafed;
> Now banifhed are the boifterous feftivals,
> The giddy dance, and they whom it hath pleafed,
> And defolation ftalketh, heart difeafed;
> And fee how folly's revelry is flown,
> Leaving behind an emptinefs, increafed
> By the dull dropping of fome crumbling ftone.
> The plafter name-affailed, and they who fcribbled gone."

A witty Frenchman has pronounced upon the many names
of unknowns to be found here as follows, on a confpicuous
part of the wall:—

" Les noms des fous
On trouve partout."

By a handfome ftaircafe, the vifitor after leaving the great
hall, reaches a fuite of rooms, ending in a bay window. But
it is not to fee thefe that he afcends ; it is to peer into the
room in which died the haplefs Princefs Elizabeth, the
innocent victim, crufhed between a king and a people in
antagonifm. It is a low fquare room, lit by the one window
under which the princefs was found dead—a defolate dungeon,
and the bedroom of a princefs. Doubtlefs the poor child was
imprifoned in this room becaufe of its fafety and feclufion.
There was no window from which an attempt could be made
to efcape, and the room was far away from the outer walls of
the caftle. The flooring is now fo dangerous that the vifitor is
not allowed to go beyond the gateway ; and one experiences a
ftrange fenfe of intrufion when looking in at the door. Between
the parted walls and ceiling the ivy has crept in to look upon
the fcene. It is pale, fickly-looking, ftraggling—indeed the
young imprifoned ivy is fingularly typical of the imprifonment
of Elizabeth Stuart, whofe fweet features in marble are to be
feen in the new church of St. Thomas à Becket, at Newport.

It is almoft a relief to quit this part of the caftle, and get
once more out into the open-air again.

And here, round the corner, is the celebrated well-houfe.
Who has not heard of the wonderful well of Carifbrook Caftle ?
of fabulous depth, and the water of which is rather expenfively
drawn up by a donkey, kept to that end. This well is comparatively modern, for tradition fpeaks of the well in the keep,
which as the citadel to which the befieged would retreat in

cafe of neceffity, had to be provided with water, happen what might. The well-houfe of the more modern well was built in the fifteenth century, but it has been reftored and repaired within the laft ten years.

Knight fays, "One of the moft curious things in the caftle is *the* other well, which is above 300 feet deep. The vifitor is fhown into the well-houfe (near the entrance); and while he is noticing the fingular appearance of the room, one fide of which is occupied by an enormous wooden wheel, a fmall lamp is lighted; and after being told to mark the time that elapfes before a glafs of water that is thrown down ftrikes againft the bottom of the well, the lamp is lowered by means of a fmall windlafs, making, as he watches its defcent, a circle of light continually leffening till the lamp is feen to float on the furface of the water, at a depth that makes him almoft dizzy. A grave old donkey is then introduced, who quietly walks into the huge treadwheel, which he anon begins to turn—as curs in days of yore turned fpits—whereby the bucket is lowered and drawn up again, which feat being accomplifhed, Jacob very foberly walks out again."

Common honefty compels us to ftate that the well is not fo deep as here ftated to be. Inclufive of the water varying from 30 to 40 feet, the depth is not more than 200. Some extraordinary tales are told of the longevity of the donkeys ufed in the well-houfe. Several are fpoken of as having worked through twenty-fix years; and an old authority fpeaks of an animal which died in 1771, after having drawn innumerable buckets of water during the forty-feven years through which it is ftated his induftry lafted.

We are bound to confefs, that from enquiries made on the fpot, we found that the average duration of a donkey's pilgrimage in the wheel is about ten years. And, furthermore, we

Y

may ftate that the donkey of this period (1868) fhowed in our prefence great intelligence by a very decided difinclination to get into the hollow drum, and a ftronger difinclination when he had been perfuaded thereto, to move on.

By the way, one of the donkeys of the dynafty was a pen-fioner of the Duke of Gloucefter, uncle of George III., who fettled on it an annuity of a penny loaf a day; a bounty which it enjoyed for many years.

As for the water, it is worth a journey to the Ifle of Wight to drink it. So pure is this fparkling natural champagne, that its frefhnefs renders it a medicinal water then and there.

And now the eye falls upon the moft picturefque flight of fteps (a mafs of beautiful broken lines—tree-fhadow and fun-fhine) that can be found even in an old Englifh caftle. 'Tis exquifite. The guide books give the exact number of fteps, 72, and if you count them you will find that the flight is one fhort. This is the way to the keep, the vital point of the caftle in the middle ages, when the beacon was lighted, and the look-out rigoroufly kept. Implacable time has left his mark upon it. The well is choked up, the terrace is bramble-grown, the roof fallen in, and yet it is only three hundred years fince moft of thefe turrets and look-outs were built. They are due to the dread of the Spanifh Armada, and the genius of Geno-bella, an Italian engineer, who took for his model the fortifica-tions of Antwerp, a city which had had much experience in fighting. That keep, which is now fo quiet, was alive with hundreds of willing workers while the panic lafted. Elizabeth contributed £4,000, the gentry of the ifland £400—not a great fum, feeing what vital interefts they had in the operations—and every man in the ifland gave his labours to it. The keep and caftle have been invaded at laft. The daws and tourifts have befieged it, and thy hold poffeffion of the ftronghold ftill.

It is poffible to make almoft the circuit of the caftle by means of the old ramparts, now narrow and weed-grown, yet ftill as firm as when firft laid—nay, firmer. Time is eating away the caftle at its edges, beautifully rounding and dimpling its face, but it has not yet torn its walls afunder.

Leaving the caftle, it is well to wander down to Carifbrook church, a noble fpecimen of Early Englifh. The cure is a vicarage, beftowed by Charles II. upon Queen's College, Oxford, and is worth over a thoufand a year. This church has a rival in the parifh called *St. Nicholas within the Caftle*, a mere finecure (in the gift of the governor), and therefore worth having, although only of the annual value of £24.

The bells of Carifbrook are eight, and very beautiful. The church contains one of thofe monuments which have ceafed to be added to in our time. It was raifed to one Captain William Keeling; he is reprefented fitting on the deck of a fhip, with a crown of glory over him. *Fides* (Faith) is written on the fail; on the compafs, *Verbum Dei* (the Word of God); and on the anchor, *Spes* (Hope). The infcription below the fhip informs us that he died in 1619. It thus quaintly concludes :—

> " FORTIE and *two* years in this veffel frail,
> On the rough fea of life did KEELING fail ;
> A merchant fortunate, a captain bould,
> A courtier gracious, yet alas! not old.
> Such wealth, experience, honor, and high praife,
> Few winne in twice fo manie years or daies ;
> But what the world admired he deemed droffe,
> For Chrift—without Chrift all his gains but loffe ;
> For him and his dear love, with merrie cheere,
> To the *Holy Land* his laft courfe he did fteere ;
> *Faith* ferved for fails—the *Sacred Word* for card,
> *Hope* was his anchor, *Glory* his reward ;
> And thus with gales of grace, by happy venter
> Thro' *ftraits* of Death—HEAVEN's *harbor* he did enter !"

In quitting Carifbrook, let us do the parliamentarians juftice by faying that there is no honeft evidence to fhow that it was ever in contemplation to apprentice the Princefs Elizabeth to a button-maker at Newport, while in reference to the caufe of her death, a recent examination of the remains proves that her end was a refult of fuch natural conftitutional decay as no treatment could have arrefted. We cannot do better than end this chapter with a copy of the princefs's account of her laft interview with her ill-fated father.

"*What the king faid to me* 29*th of January laft, being the laft time I had the happinefs to fee him.*

" He told me that he was glad I was come, for, though he had not time to fay much, yet fomewhat he wifhed to fay to me, which he could not to another, and he had feared 'the cruelty' was too great to permit his writing. ' But fweetheart,' he added, ' thou wilt forget what I tell thee.' Then fhedding abundance of tears, I told him I would write down all he faid to me. ' He wifhed me,' he faid, ' not to grieve and torment myfelf for him, for it was a glorious death he fhould die, it being for the laws and religion of the land.' He told me what books to read againft Popery. He faid, that ' he had forgiven all his enemies, and he hoped God would forgive them alfo;' and he commanded us, and all the reft of my brothers and fifters to forgive them alfo. Above all, he bade me tell my mother that ' his thoughts had never ftrayed from her, and that his love for her would be the fame to the laft;' withal, he commanded me and my brother to love her, and be obedient to her. He defired me ' not to grieve for him, for he fhould die a martyr; and that he doubted not but God would reftore the throne to his fon, and that then we fhould be all happier than we poffibly could have been, if he had lived;' with many other things, which I cannot remember.

" Then, taking my brother Gloucefter on his knee, he faid, ' Sweetheart, now will they cut off thy father's head ;' upon which the child looked very fteadfaftly upon him. ' Heed, my child, what I fay; they will cut off my head, and perhaps make thee a king. But mark what I fay : you muft not be a king as long as your brothers Charles and James live; therefore I charge you, do not be made king by them.' At which the child, fighing deeply, replied, ' I will be torn in pieces firft.' And thefe words coming from fo young a child, rejoiced my father exceedingly; and his majefty fpoke to him of the welfare of his foul, and to keep his religion, commanding him to fear God and He would provide for him. All which the young child earneftly promifed.

" His majefty alfo bid me fend his bleffing to the reft of my brothers and fifters. So after giving me his bleffing, I took my leave."

And fo we take leave of Carifbrook.

> " Time, by his gradual touch,
> Has moulder'd into beauty many a tower,
> Which, when it frown'd with all its battlements,
> Was only terrible."

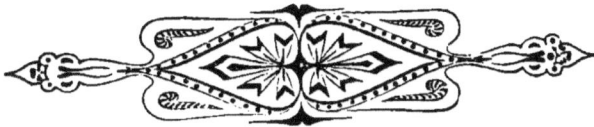

Environs of Carifbrook and Newport.

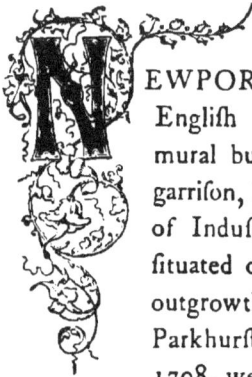

N EWPORT having been one of the firft towns in Englifh hiftory to difcover the value of extramural burial, it is quite natural to find that its garrifon, its prifon, and its union, or rather Houfe of Induftry (a far lefs formidable title), are all fituated outfide the town. The prifon was the outgrowth of the barracks, which, eftablifhed at Parkhurft, a mile and a half from Newport, in 1798, were named after the fite, until they were changed to the Albany, in honour of the commander-in-chief, the Duke of York and Albany. It is faid that the arrangements at thefe barracks are only furpaffed by the fyftem in operation at Woolwich. There is accommodation for about 2,000 men.

It was only fo late as 1838 that the prifon was eftablifhed. The fcheme was for the formation of a reformatory for juvenile offenders. In fact, this jail was one of the very earlieft reformatories organifed. A fecond prifon, for adult offenders, was afterwards added. Thefe together offer accommodation for 700 prifoners, which is, however, rarely accepted by more than 400 at any one time. The fyftem in ufe in both prifons is rather conciliatory than coercive, and it has been attended with really fatisfactory refults. The endeavour to counteract crime through the medium of education has here had a marked fuccefs.

The trio of public buildings at Parkhurft is completed by the Houfe of Induftry, which, eftablifhed in 1790, is conducted under a local act. There can be little doubt that the fyftem purfued here, as the name indicates, is one which anticipated the fcheme which in recent years has been gradually and fuccefsfully applied to the workhoufes of England—a fcheme which endeavours to make the union fyftem in fome degree felf-fupporting. The Houfe of Induftry will contain 700 guefts, but, like its neighbour, the prifon, is rarely patronized by more than 400. It is furrounded by a garden farm of eighty acres, which is kept in good order by the inmates; the younger of whom are taught various trades in fhops forming part of the eftablifhment, the produce of the manufactured goods from which forms not a fmall item in the income of the place.

Thorne fays of the adjacent fcenery:—"The country around Carifbrook is very lovely. There are delicious green lanes, where the trees interlace overhead and form an exquifite roof to the informal avenue; there are again lone farm-houfes, fhaded by lofty fpreading elms, and environed by broad tilths of wheat; little playful brooks running wild among the alder fpotted meadows, and downy heights with wide-fpread profpects, and fhadowy copfes, peopled only by the merry fong-birds. You might roam about here for weeks, and not exhauft the affluence of gentle paftoral lovelinefs."

Newtown is fome miles from Newport, but to the politician
it is worth a mufing vifit.   An extract from an old account
of the Ifle of Wight will give an idea of what Newtown
was:—"This town derives its name from the circumftance
of its being rebuilt after its deftruction by the French in the
reign of Richard the Second.   It is very fmall, reduced to
about a dozen *cottages*, though it was formerly of confiderable
extent, and it is deemed to be one of the moft ancient places in
the ifland.   The town-hall ftands on an eminence overlooking
the harbour.   In the principal room are oaken chairs, curioufly
carved in the time of Queen Befs of profperous memory.   It
is a chapelry to the mother church.   The haven is the beft in
the ifland.   At high water veffels of confiderable tonnage may
ride there with the utmoft fafety.   The town has a corporation
of mayor and burgeffes ; but what is fomewhat remarkable, this
body does not confift of the inhabitants, but of the proprietors
of certain tenures, which entitle them to a vote in the election
of two members of parliament.   Thus like Old Sarum, it has
its portion in the legiflature of Great Britain."

Now Newtown is what it fhould be.   The Reform Act
fwept it away nearly forty years fince.   It is a little faded,
fleepy, broken-down village.   And once it was the chief place
on the ifland, and returned two members to Parliament.

And while at Newport the vifitor fhould give an hour to
Gatcomb, for in its church, dedicated to St. Olave, is to be
found, on the north fide of the chancel, the figure of a man
carved in wood, which is called the old wooden faint, but is
probably a reprefentation of one of the family of the Lifles.   In
fact, the figure is that of a Knight Templar, very remarkable
from being accompanied by a dwarf winged angel, or good
genius, watching at the fhoulder ; the idea of which moft
certainly came from the Eaft with the Crufaders.

Shorwell.

—◇◇◇—

LEAVING Blackgang behind him, the tourist
may now take the military road which runs in a
direct line to Freshwater. It is a desolate road.
War having fortunately been absent, the weeds
have sprung up apace, and one shall find thistles
six feet in height. Such a sight would be a
melancholy one were the road a road of peace;
but being what it is, a highway of war, may the
thistles flourish! As a mere means of communication, nothing can be more objectionable than
this military road. Walking on shingle were far
preferable. Certainly in parts this structure rises to the heroic.
Some of the viaducts over the chines which cut it at right
angles are almost Roman in their scope and style.

If we break away from this direct but stony highway, and
face to the right, we shall reach the charming village of Shorwell, a perfect nest of ruralities.

Shorwell is the paradife of fhady lanes, while its church—
not very important in itfelf, although it contains one or two
interefting braffes—is rendered charming by its fetting of trees.
In the high noon of fummer one has never far to go to find
fhade in Shorwell. It is a village park. In addition to the
church, our artift has chofen for illuftration one of thefe
Shorwell lanes—its moffy banks thick with ferns and flowers,
and the branches meeting overhead.

LANE AT SHORWELL.

FRESHWATER BAY

Freſhwater.

———◆———

FRESHWATER, rendered famous by the reſidence of the poet Tennyſon, is the moſt rural of the great ſea-bathing points in the iſland—its trelliſed houſes are a ſight to ſee.

Moſt people who viſit Freſhwater aſk for the houſe of the poet. It is ſo buried in trees that it cannot be ſeen except by treſpaſſing, of which it is ſaid the poet ſo bitterly complains that he had it ſome time ſince in contemplation to quit the iſland. But we venture to ſuppoſe that many of thoſe who may be ſuddenly eſpied from Farringford ſtrolling up the ſweep to the houſe, are not ſo much treſpaſſers as unintentional offenders, who find the gate open, and take the road for a public one, the poet not having put up an intimation that the grounds are private.

"And have you ever ſeen Mr. Tennyſon?" we aſk a little girl.

"Oh yes, Sir. He goes about by himſelf in the lanes, with a great big brown hat on."

But to return to the defcription of Frefhwater Bay and Cliffs.
An old authority fays:—" Thefe cliffs are remarkable for the
prodigious numbers of aquatic birds which frequent them, more
particularly reforting there from May to Auguft, to depofit their
eggs amongft the crevices between the fhelving ftrata, at a great
height, and yet confiderably below the fummit of thefe perpendicular precipices.   Here many perfons of the neighbourhood
annually rifk their lives in the terrific adventure of taking the
eggs, which are much efteemed, and deftroying the birds to
obtain the feathers, which are of the foft quality called eider.
A dozen birds generally yield one pound weight of foft feathers,
for which the merchants give eightpence ; the carcaffes are
bought by the fifhermen at fixpence per dozen, for the purpofe
of baiting their crab-pots.

"An iron crow is firmly driven into the ground at the fummit,
and a ftout rope turned round it: the adventurer placing himfelf
aftride a piece of wood, fufpended by one end of the rope, and
faftening or lowering at pleafure, the other part of the rope, by
letting it flip over the iron, he thus defcends gradually to whatever point of the precipice he wifhes to explore ; and in the
end afcends in the fame manner, or is drawn up by his confede-
rates; raifing in the breaft of the fpectator tremendous fenfations!

" An awful example of danger attending this adventure has
this year occurred : an artillery foldier, from one of the neighbouring barracks, without experience, and it fhould feem without
proper caution, attempted it alone, and is fuppofed to have neglected to faften the rope about his body ; however this might
be, he was feen by the party at the fignal-houfe to fall headlong,
dafhing from crag to crag ; and his mutilated remains were
found a horrible fpectacle among the rocks at the bottom of
the cliff."

A later account gives the following lift of various birds to be feen on thefe rocks in May, June, and July :—Puffins, gulls, cormorants, choughs, eider ducks, auks, divers, guillemots, razor bills, widgeons, willocks, daws, ftarlings, and pigeons.

Recent tourifts (ourfelves amongft the number) have watched in June and July for thefe birds, and feen not a fpecimen. Thus it is that one traveller and another differ fo widely.

Frefhwater Cave can only be entered at low water; it is an excavation made beneath a lofty cliff, by the conftant affaults of the fea; the entrance is rather narrow, but the depth is forty yards. This cave, opening under the cliff, expands into a marine grotto of confiderable dimenfions, and forms an interefting and impreffive object to the curious traveller. A flight pier of chalk divides the mouth of the cave into two unequal arches, beyond the fmaller of which is another of the fame fize. The principal arch is between twenty and thirty feet in height.

The fea-view from the upper part of the cave, with its wild fore-ground, formed by large fragments of the rock, which lie fcattered before the fpectator, is ftrikingly beautiful. Through the leffer opening are feen the oppofite cliffs of Frefhwater Bay; while the main arch difplays a wide expanfe of ocean, and in the diftance, the noble fummit of St. Catherine's Hill. The floor of the cave is a clear pebbly beach, ftrewn with maffes of the rock of every fize and fhape.

Another of the curiofities is the arched rock which ftands on the eaftern fide of the bay. It is a very large mafs of chalk, which has been originally part of the cliff, but now ftands infulated in the fea, fome fix hundred feet from it. The fame power that deftroyed the intervening cliff has beaten a way through this rock, in the fhape of a rude Gothic arch; the furface of the rock is ftrangely worn and fhattered: it has altogether a curious appearance, which is confiderably increafed if the fea-fowl be difturbed that rooft about its ledges in vaft numbers. There is another, but more lumpifh mafs rifing out of the fea at a little diftance from the Arched Rock.

And now you can mount the cliffs, and continue along their fummit to the Needles. The walk is a moft exhilarating one. The view acrofs the fea is glorious, and the balmy breezes come over the wide waters with that delightful frefhnefs which is never felt but in wandering along the lofty hills that rife at once from the broad ocean. The Downs are open, and only employed for grazing fheep; you may therefore make your own path over them, as the lighthoufe is a fufficient landmark. The cliffs here rife precipitoufly from the fea; and they are the higheft chalk cliffs in the kingdom. At High Down they attain an altitude of above fix hundred feet. Samphire grows abundantly on thefe cliffs, and is in common ufe as a pickle among the poorer claffes.

The lighthoufe, which originally ftood on the brow of the hill above the Needles, has recently been removed to the bafe of one of the rocks, as fhown in our illuftration. In its place is one of thofe forts, now difagreeably numerous on the ifland, which were built in confequence of the invafion panic a few years ago. Permiffion is readily given to pafs through the fort to the extreme point of the ifland, whence there is an excellent view to be obtained of Scratchell's Cave and Bay.

Scratchell's Bay.

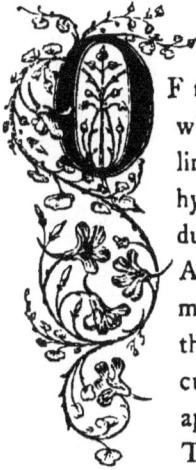

O F this beautiful fpot Mantell fays:—"The pure
white chalk of Scratchell's Bay is compofed of
lime and carbonic acid. It diffolves rapidly in
hydro-chloric acid, and leaves only a flight refi-
duum confifting of filex and organic matter.
A microfcopical examination fhows it to be a
mere aggregation of fhells and corals, fo minute
that upwards of a million are contained in a
cubic inch of chalk. The amorphous particles
appear to be the detritus of fimilar ftruftures.
Thefe organifms, for the moft part, are the
calcareous fhields and chambered fhells of the animalcules,
termed *foraminifera*, which fwarm in inconceivable numbers in
our prefent feas, and are daily and hourly contributing to the
amount of fediment now forming in the bed of the ocean. The
nodules and veins of flint that are fo abundant in the upper
chalk, have probably been produced by the agency of heated
water and vapours. The perfeft fluidity of the filiceous matter
before its confolidation is proved, not only by the fharp moulds

and impreſſions of ſhells retained by the flints, but alſo by the preſence of numerous organic bodies in the ſubſtance of the nodular maſſes, and the ſilicified condition of the ſponges and other zoophytes, which ſwarm in ſome of the cretaceous ſtrata.

" Although ſilex, or the earth of flint, is inſoluble in water at the ordinary temperature, its ſolution readily takes place in vapour heated a little above that of caſt iron; and this has been proved by actual experiment. Similar effects are being produced at the preſent moment by natural cauſes. The ſiliceous depoſits formed by the intermittent boiling fountains, called the geyſers, in Iceland, are well known ; and in New Zealand this phenomenon is exhibited on a ſtill larger ſcale.

" The moſt ſtupendous line of chalk cliffs in this diſtrict is that termed the Main-bench, Then follows Scratchell's Bay, which is terminated by the Needles. The aſpect of this bay is romantic in the extreme. In the face of the cliff, from the deſtruction of the lower beds of the bent ſtrata, a magnificent arch, 300 feet high, has been produced, and forms an alcove that overhangs the beach 150 feet.

" The well-known pinnacles of chalk, called The Needles, are iſolated maſſes at the extreme weſtern point of the middle range of downs, which have been produced by the decompoſition and wearing away of the rock in the direction of the joints or fiſſures by which the ſtrata are traverſed. The angular or wedge-ſhaped form of theſe rocks has reſulted from the highly-inclined northward dip of the beds of which they are compoſed."

To the late Sir Henry Englefield belongs the great merit of having firſt obſerved and directed attention to the intereſting phenomena occaſioned by this diſruption and elevation of the eocene and cretaceous formations, which are ſo remarkably diſplayed in the Iſle of Wight; namely, the vertical poſition of the ſtrata, and the ſhattered condition of the flint nodules, though ftill embedded in the folid rock. Thefe appearances are very readily examined at Scratchell's Bay. The chalk forms parallel beds or ftrata, varying from two to five feet in thicknefs, which are commonly feparated by layers of flint nodules, embedded at irregular diftances from each other. There are alfo a few nodules difperfed indifcriminately in the mafs. The dip of the inclined ftrata is in general from 70° to 80°, but many beds in the ifle are quite vertical. The parallelifm of the cretaceous ftrata, and the abfence of fand, gravel, and other coarfe detritus, denote that the depofition of thefe calcareous fediments took place in tranquil water, and remote from feacliffs and fhores. Where a large extent of the cliff is expofed, the face of the chalk is feen to be traverfed by fiffures or joints at right angles to the planes of ftratification.

Upon carefully extricating a flint nodule from this cliff, it retains its original form. But upon examination it will be found fhattered in every direction, and broken into pieces varying in fize from three inches in diameter down to the minuteft fragment, and even into an impalpable powder. The flints thus fhattered, as if by a blow of inconceivable force, retain their form and pofition in the bed. The chalk clofely invefts them on every fide, and until removed nothing different from other flints can be perceived, except fine lines indicating the fracture, as in broken glafs. But when moved, they fall at once to pieces. The fragments are as fharp as poffible, and quite irregular, being certainly not the effect of any peculiar cryftallization or internal arrangement of the material, but folely attributable to external violence.

Sir Henry Englefield concludes that this fhattered condition of the flints has arifen from the concuffion caufed by the upheaval and difruption of the once horizontal depofits.

No one fhould mifs Scratchell's Bay. The clearnefs of the

A A

water here is marvellous, while the fcene, as viewed from the back of the cave, and framed in by its height, is magnificent. Only under thefe circumftances are the Needles feen at their beft. Here " veins of rock, fhooting from the cliffs, run to a length that cannot be afcertained, terminating in the fea. At a diftance they appear like water pipes, and on examination, are found to confift, in the middle, of a vein of black rock, covered with an incruftation of iron. The fhape of thefe veins is fingular, but very regular and pointed ; they dart into the fea among the other rocks, which form the entrance of Frefhwater Cave. The Needle Cave is 300 feet deep."

Yarmouth.

A FEW words concerning Yarmouth, and we fhall
have fpoken of every place of importance on the
coaft of this ifland. From Yarmouth you mark
Hurft Caftle, almoft an ifland of itfelf, where
Charles I. was confined when the Parliamentarians feared that the fallen king might efcape from
the Ifle of Wight if he were not removed from
Carifbrook.

Even an inhabitant of the ifle, and one of its devoted fons,
can find nothing better to fay of Yarmouth than this :—" The
only place of any importance in the weft of the ifland is Yarmouth, which is ten miles diftant from Newport. The number
of inhabitants in the town and parifh is 650. The town of
Yarmouth, which was anciently called *Eremuth*, is of confiderable antiquity, and contains feveral ftreets of well-built houfes ;
one of which, at the north-weft corner of the town, adjoining
the quay, was built by Lord Holmes at the time he was
Governor of the Ifland ; and here he entertained Charles the
Second when he vifited Yarmouth. It fhared the fate of

Newtown in the firſt year of Richard II., having been deſtroyed
by the French in 1377. In the time of Edward the Third,
Yarmouth was one of the licenſed ports. There is not much
buſineſs carried on in the town ; but veſſels occaſionally bring
up in the roads, if the wind prevents their getting round the
Needles. It was formerly much larger, as the ſites of ſeveral
old ſtreets can be clearly traced."

The Yarmouth boatmen are celebrated for pluck, and it is
pleaſant to ſee them actively preparing to go to ſea. We are
watching a light-built cutter preparing to run out from the
harbour, when one who has been a good ſailor in the heyday
of youth, but who is now old, takes his place at our elbow.
The men miſcalculate, and in trying to make the mouth of
the harbour, the boat is ſent a point or two to leeward, and
her bow is ſplintered upon certain ſtone-work.

"Ha !" we ſay, "thought ſhe would ſtrike the wall."

"Wall, Sir," ſays the diſguſted tar at our ſide, "that's the
CASTLE."

A wall, we declare, not much higher than the quays, and this
is the celebrated Yarmouth Caſtle, built by Henry VIII. It
looks like the back-yard of the George Inn, a fine, handſome
Elizabethan building, once the reſidence of Sir Robert Holmes.

Says one of the authorities :—" The caſtle is ſituated on the
extreme point of land on the eaſt ſide of the Yar ; it was erected
by Henry VIII., on the ſite of a church which had recently
been deſtroyed by the French. The expenſes of its buildings
were defrayed out of the religious houſes which that monarch
diſſolved. The fortification conſiſts of a platform with eight
guns, which commands the narrow channel between the town
and Hurſt Caſtle. To the northward of the caſtle is a platform
with large guns." It was much ſtrengthened in 1855.

"The firſt charter of franchiſe was granted to the town by

Baldwin, Earl of Devonshire, and Lord of the Isle of Wight, in 1135, the 36th year of the reign of Henry I., and it was confirmed by Edward I., Henry VI., Edward IV., and Queen Elizabeth. It was re-incorporated by James I., in the year 1608, the seventh year of his reign. This borough sent two members to Parliament; a privilege it first exercised the 23rd of Edward I., in 1304, and was the first town in the island selected for that honour. It is a curious fact that although several writs were afterwards directed to Yarmouth, it does not appear that any members were returned until the 27th of Elizabeth (1584), when it was again summoned, since which time it has been regularly represented until 1832, when, by the passing of the Reform Act, it was disfranchised.

"The elective franchise was vested in the Mayor and Corporation. The greatest number of votes polled at any election during the previous thirty years was nine. It is not necessary to reside in the town or neighbourhood to enjoy the dignified and honourable office of Mayor."

Yarmouth is one of the towns where the carol lingers upon New-year's day, the children have an outing, and sing as follows:

> " Waffail, waffail to our town !
> The cup is white and the ale is brown ;
> The cup is made of the ashen tree,
> And so is the ale of good barley.
> Little maid, little maid, turn the pin,
> Open the door, and let me come in.
> Joy be there and joy be here,
> We wish you all a happy New Year!"

Crossing the harbour, we arrive at Norton, a pleasant village on the opposite side of the river, where there are several delightful villas and cottages. A walk from here to the Downs will repay the labour by the beauty of the scenery. To the westward, on Norton Common, opposite to Hurst Castle, are the

fites of Carey's Sconce, and Worfley's Tower, two fortifications
fucceffively erected near the fame fpot, in the reigns of Henry
VIII. and Elizabeth, for the defence of the narrow fea.

At the turning of Sconce Point we reach Colwell Bay,
where once again the Needles come into view.

Not far from Yarmouth is Shalfleet, celebrated for a heavy
Norman church, in the graveyard of which is to be found a
quaint and cynical epitaph :—

> " His change I hope is for the beft;
> He is with Jefus, or at reft."

The church is an ancient and fingular ftructure. It confifts
of a body, chancel, and fouth aifle, with a low tower. The
north porch is of Norman architecture, embellifhed with a rude
fculpture of a bifhop, the arms extended, and the hands refting
on animals refembling griffins. The windows were formerly
ornamented with painted glafs; the arms of Montacute Earl of
Salifbury, and of Ifabella de Fortibus, ftill remain in them.

www.ingramcontent.com/pod-product-compliance
Lightning Source LLC
Chambersburg PA
CBHW030830270326

41928CB00007B/984